The History *of* Pierce Pond

The History *of* Pierce Pond

by Gary Cobb
and Alfred H. Fenton

This edition,
limited to 2,000 copies,
was printed by
Knowlton & McLeary,
Farmington, Maine
in March of 1992.

500 copies are numbered and
signed by the authors.

This is Number

Dedication

This volume is dedicated to the Pierce Pond Family, those hundreds of men, women and children who, over the years, have made Pierce Pond an idyllic and idealistic retreat that cleanses the mind and refurbishes the soul.

Pierce Pond is almost a religion. Certainly there are those who worship the place and this fervor has been created by the combined efforts and attitudes of every category of person involved in the operation, be he man or woman, guide or guest, owner or helper, cook or bottle washer, neophyte or foxy grandpa.

To each and every one of you, thanks for being a dedicated Pierce Ponder. This is for you.

Gary Cobb
North New Portland
August 1991

Contents

Foreword

In the spring of 1989 Gary Cobb asked me to look over the history of Pierce Pond Camps which he had started. I became intrigued and went home to Brunswick to see what material I might find in the Bowdoin College Library. I examined every item in its Maine collection, including publications of the several railroads in the state which were issued at the turn of the century. I also read the reports of the Maine Fish Commission from 1867 to the present and discovered that anything that Gary and I turned out would have to cover a wider range than Pierce Pond Township.

It was not until the spring of 1990, however, that I realized that it would take an outsider to capture the flavor of the Pierce Pond operation. On my annual trip to the pond I was able to get closer to the spirit of the place. I passed up most of my fishing opportunities in order to concentrate on the history and by keeping close to Gary and Betty and the crew in the kitchen I came to see that there was no way in which Gary could write about his family so as to bring out their true essence.

For example, one afternoon I heard one side of a telephone

conversation Gary had. An elderly guest from Anson was calling to say that circumstances prevented him from honoring his reservation. Gary was most sympathetic and responded:

"You would eat a trout if someone were to deliver it to you, wouldn't you?"

The answer obviously was yes and after hanging up the receiver, Gary remarked to Betty:

"Remind me to get a trout and take it down to Mr. X in Anson."

There is no way Gary Cobb would ever commit such an incident to paper.

There have been four generations of Cobbs involved with Pierce Pond Camps and the spell they have cast over the operation is not likely to be broken for some time. Maude Cobb set the pace in 1958 when she and Floyd took over the business. She treated her guests as though they were family, and the help, well, it was virtually family anyway. Gary and Betty have carried on in the same tradition. Pierce Pond Camps have become a home in the woods for hundreds of grateful men and women and the Cobbs have reaped their gratitude. The camps are a homestead to which succeeding generations return joyfully each season.

Romeo St. John, the 78-year-old gatekeeper who has spent his life in the Maine woods and has known a multitude of bosses, good and bad, has this to say about the Cobbs:

"They use me good."

Alfred H. Fenton
Brunswick, Maine
June, 1991

Sources and Acknowledgments

What started out as an innocent history of Pierce Pond Camps in time developed into an examination of much that has happened in the Upper Kennebec Valley and other remote portions of the State of Maine over the years. As the nineteenth century evolved into the twentieth, the lumbering industry, the railroads and recreational fishing and hunting blended together into a whirlpool of activity. Investigation of the one facet led quickly into another, so that this final product is a collage of facts, figures and fiction gathered from files, microfiche, books, pamphlets, microfilm, old wives' tales, diaries, court records, and the memories of many of those involved in the care and feeding of sports in general and at Pierce Pond in particular.

There is much good material available on the history of the Upper Kennebec Valley from Father Rale's diaries covering his life at Madison with the Kennebecs, to the more recent works of Mary R. Calvert. As John Farrar, the New York publisher, once wrote a writer in his stable: "The Indians will get you if you don't watch out." And if anyone cares to get involved with them, the six-volume treatise on the American

Indian by Henry Schoolcraft will keep you busy for at least a year.

Equally detailed are two volumes published by the Colonial Society of Massachusetts entitled *William Bingham's Maine Lands*. As with most scholarly works this history of the Million Acres is heavy sledding, but profitable.

The bulk of the information used in this present volume came from the Bowdoin College Library and the University of Maine Library at Farmington. At Bowdoin was found the complete set of reports of the Maine Fish Commission, later to be known as the Department of Inland Fisheries and Game. The earlier reports, beginning in 1867, are especially helpful in describing the status of salmon fishing in Maine rivers, B.D. and A.D., Before Dams and After Dams. They also reveal how quickly the Maine Fish Commission placed emphasis on rearing and stocking game fish for the benefit of the thousands of sportsmen who had discovered the joys of angling for trout and salmon in Maine. In this connection we wish to express our thanks to Mr. John Ladley, Jr., Mrs. Laura McCourt and Mrs. Elda Takagi for their cheerful and most helpful assistance in steering us to the material we required.

The Farmington Library has a complete file of the publication, *Maine Woods,* a weekly newspaper published at Philips from 1879 to 1913, and from this medium, which glorified and perhaps deified life in the Maine woods, Gary Cobb extracted a bountiful crop of specifics about the goings on at the numerous sporting camps along the Kennebec and Dead Rivers.

Individuals who contributed substantially to our efforts include Charlie Abbe; Leon Baril, manager of East Carry Pond

Camps, who made available his register; Charles Cleaver; Bob Estes, former woods boss for Great Northern Paper Company; Doris Grieves, widow of Perry, who preceded the Cobbs as operators of the camps; Lester and Villa Lawyerson of Bingham, long-time employees; Howard Mitchell, son of a former co-owner; Mrs. J. Ramos and Muriel Humphreys Willeford, grand-daughters of C. S. Humphreys; the late Armond Spalding, son of the founder of Pierce Pond Camps; Richard Spalding, who made available the diary of his grandfather, Charles Spalding; and numerous Pierce Pond guests, especially such old-timers as Morgan Daboll, Emile Gaulien, Dick Fagan, Doug and Louise Allen, and Bob Witbeck.

Others who were interviewed and made equally valuable contributions of information about events and people include Azel Adams, Louise Belanger, Sally Butcher, Mrs. Sidney Cadwallader, Alice Bean Kennedy Giradin, Ella Palmer, Nellie Macdougall Parks, Louise Sterling Pierce, Ken Taylor, Bob Viles, Olive Smith, and Duluth Wing.

On the production end we must give special thanks to Walter P. Bowman, professor Emeritus of English at the New York State University at Brockport, for a scholarly and sometimes embarrassing thoroughness in smoothing out the verbiage of this volume, as well as to Peter L. Fenton who read the final manuscript. Equally important has been the contribution of Nancy H. Fenton, former production chief for Silver Burdett & Ginn. Nancy not only typed the manuscript into a computer, but also designed the volume and saw it through to press. The charts in the Appendix were prepared by Pamela Donahue.

Our gratitude must also be expressed to our wives, relatives and friends who tolerated us during more than two years of concentration that excluded all ordinary activities pertaining to daily life. Like lovers, authors are completely oblivious to much of what goes on around them. They live in another world, in this case that of the golden days of fishing and hunting in the Maine of 100 years ago. How often have people wondered what life was like before civilization began to get in the way of the individual? We have luxuriated in that world vicariously and found it good. We hope we have given you a glimpse of what it was like.

Gary Cobb
Alfred H. Fenton

Chronology

1775	Benedict Arnold marches troops through the Carry Pond area.
1795	William Bingham makes million-acre Kennebec Purchase from General Henry Knox.
1817	Old Canada Road laid out and swamped.
1820 (circa)	Pierce Pond gets its name.
1832	Emerson Dam constructed.
1894	Pierce Pond receives secret stocking of land locked salmon and trout.
1900 (circa)	Sporting camps established at Otter Pond, Black Brook, Spring Lake and Rowe Ponds; Rance Ham catches 16-pound salmon.
1903	Henry Lane erects cabin on Pierce Pond; Pierce Pond Fish and Game Association of Madison founded, builds cabin at Pierce Pond.
1904	Charles Spalding takes over cabins on Pierce Pond and begins operation of a sporting camp; Pierce Pond receives stocking of Quinnat salmon.

1910	Holbrook cabin built on island opposite Pierce Pond Camps.
1919	Smith camp built on cliff opposite Pierce Pond Camps; Armond Spalding takes over operation of camps.
1920	James Kelleher purchases Pierce Pond Camps.
1921	Charles Mitchell group assumes ownership of camps.
1934	Sterling Camps built on Pierce Pond Stream.
1944	Harrimans take over Pierce Pond Camps.
1947	Grieves become owners and operators.
1951	Great Northern Paper Company builds road from south to Lindsay Cove.
1952	Fire consumes 1,500 acres of woodland to west and south of camps.
1957	Bob Estes builds cabin on south shore of pond.
1958	Maude and Floyd Cobb buy Pierce Pond Camps.
1965	Fishing restrictions placed on Pierce and out-lying ponds.
1969	Wilderness Bound Camp for boys established.
1975	Bud and Dori Williams buy Sterling Camps and rename them Carrying Place Camps.
1982	Gary and Betty Cobb assume command of Pierce Pond Camps.
1986	Wilderness Bound Camps closed; Tim and Fran Harrison take over Carrying Place (Sterling) Camps and rename them Harrison's Pierce Pond Camps.

1989   Maine Wilderness Watershed Trust organized.

1990   Easement signed by Watershed Trust with Penntech Corporation thereby protecting eastern shore of Pierce Pond from development.

1991   Charlie and Trudy Valentine purchase Penntech Property.

Nota Bene

There were at least ten logging camps (marked *x* on the map facing the first chapter) established in the area represented by this map, all by lumbermen from Caratunk and environs. John Lindsay gave his name to Lindsay Cove and later Sherm Bean operated there as well as at High Pond. Hosea Bean's camps were at the Thoroughfare and Anthony Comber's on the Upper Pond. Fred and Oscar Clark logged Bowtown and the cabins they put on Otter Pond became the Otter Pond Camps.

The six homesteads shown near the Kennebec River no longer exist. They were abandoned by the mid-1920's. The site nearest Pierce Pond Stream was settled by Nathanial Pierce. Next to him was the Dexter Meservey home, later known as the Adams Farm. Then came the Tom Morris house, later to become the Spalding place. His grandson, Eldon, lives at Caratunk and remembers when the family last crossed the Kennebec in 1926. The fourth homestead was that of Robert Lawyerson, father of Lesca, the guide. Robert at one time operated a ferry from this site. The fifth and sixth homesteads were those of Alonzo Bragg and Hosea Bean. The latter was the site of a ferry as was the homestead of Tom Morris. Another ferry, not shown on the map, was operated by the Withams just below Pierce Pond Stream.

Dave Pooler, guide, builder, gatekeeper and general handyman is said to have lived in virtually every one of those houses. In fact, the story goes that he moved so often that his chickens became so accustomed to change that they would lie down to have their legs tied. When Dave's family lived in the Hosea Bean place, diphtheria struck hard and five of Dave's sisters and brothers died in as many days.

The exact route of the Canada Road from East Carry Pond to Pierce Pond is not known. It is likely that it closely followed the Carry Pond Trail, which in turn has become the Appalachian Trail of today. When the General Assembly authorized the building of the road in 1826, the job of locating it was given to one Caleb Jewett who realized $162.33 for his efforts. Undoubtedly he avoided the steep slopes of Bates Ridge and chose the notch between the ridges.

The four carries on the map connecting the Carry Ponds is the approximate route that General Benedict Arnold chose for his trek to Quebec in 1775.

The map on the following page was drawn by Clarence R. "Charlie" Gilman, a native of Bingham and a trained forester, now affiliated with the Topographic Division of the U. S. Geological Survey. In his youth he was a guide and worked briefly at the Sterling Camps.

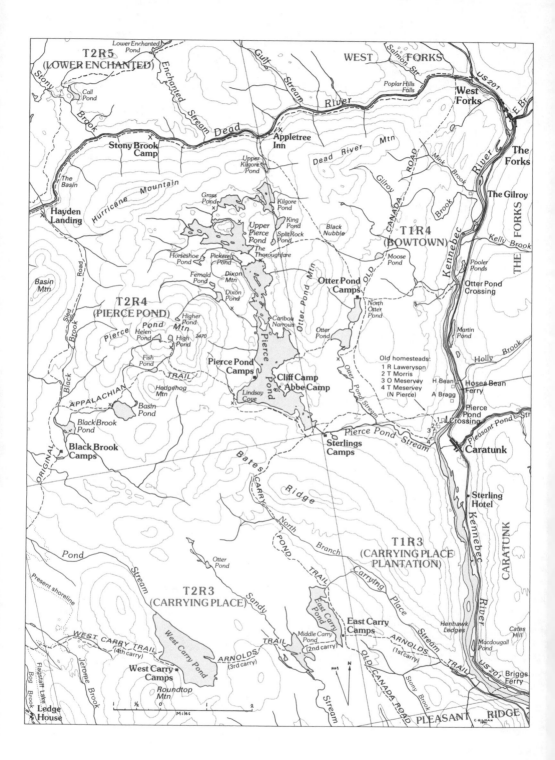

The Geology

Pierce Pond and the surrounding area inherited their good looks from their geological past, which goes back a billion years. In that period the lava that oozed out of the earth's crust was scoured by five glaciers, the last of which appeared some 25,000 years ago. What were once high, jagged mountains were scraped and rounded by the immense Laurentide ice sheet that inched its way southward from northern Canada.

The slow-moving glacier acted like a giant plow, creating furrows, gullies and shelves on the mountains. It scooped out ravines, basins and cavities which would later become ponds and lakes. During this time, Maine was buried under ice more than a mile thick. The enormous weight caused the earth's crust to sink. In places in central Maine the surface was depressed as much as 2000 feet below its present level. This allowed the sea to pour in over Maine reaching as far as Bingham. The high hills and mountains remained as islands until the earth finally rebounded and stabilized to its present level.

The mile-high ice cap began to shrink approximately 13,000 years ago. Water rushed from the bottom of the melting ice to fill the basins and cavities. The retreat turned up huge pieces of bedrock, and cracked the hard gabbro, leaving it in chunks and crags along the edges of the basins. Enormous windrows of gravel, rubble and rock were piled by the melting mass. As a result of the glacial movement, the mountains were left with a more gradual terrain on the north slopes and a steep, ledgy terrain facing the south. Good examples are the southern ledges of Moxie, Otter Pond Mountain, Bigelow and Granny's Cap.

The cavities and basins filled from the melt, then ran over, flowing from one to the other, finally filling a major basin. This in turn would overflow and cascade down the mountainside to the main flow, the Kennebec. Under and around the new basins, water burst out of the ground, insuring a continuous source of cold spring water to keep the basins filled and flowing. These became beautiful ponds like Dixon, High, Splitrock and Pierce. Anyone visiting Pierce Pond may wonder if this glacial creation were indeed governed by a supreme force. The setting could not have been arranged more picturesquely.

Eventually, some 10,000 years ago, life was restored and the slow process of evolution began. The bare terrain gradually became covered with a tundra of grasses, ferns, mosses and bush shrubs; over the following thousands of years the forest filled in. It was much like the reclamation process that follows a forest fire. First came the birch, followed by the pines, spruces and firs. The evergreens eventually gave way to the slower-growing maple, ash, oak and beech. At last, the vast forests stabilized and prevailed. The hillsides were covered with a canopy of huge hemlocks and hardwoods. As one giant tree would finally fall from old age, another would take its place.

As the vegetation continued to change, so did the animal life. This is still happening. The changes are more rapid today, as man can alter the environment practically overnight. For example, what is good habitat for deer can, in a very short time, become intolerable for them. Centuries ago this process was slow and gradual.

The white pines were the granddaddies of the forest. They were also the most useful and famous of all the trees. They stood as sentinels at each and every point, growing to a height of 200 feet, and reaching up to ten feet in diameter. They were quickly appropriated by the King of England as masts for his navy.

Next to the pines, in grandeur, were the spruce, which have the amazing ability to grow at high altitudes and perch on and about very steep ledges. They account for a big percentage of the forest from the shores to the base of the ridges, then are seen as isolated patches of green scattered on the hillsides, and lastly as the final green cap on the very top.

As with the white pine there often was one lone, majestic sentry standing on the very point of a ridge. One such sentinel stood on the south tip of Pierce Pond Mountain until the fire of 1952. Woods boss Bob Estes, who tried to save it, estimated that it was 12 feet in circumference, more than 100 feet high, and had an eagle's nest in the top. He said a pair of eagles circled continuously throughout the fire.

The ridges around Pierce Pond have remained largely untouched until very recently. In some cases during this century, the yellow birch has been cut for veneer, but many of the ridges are still in their growth stage.

The Indians

The contours sculpted by nature in pre-historic times have a definite bearing on the history of Pierce Pond Camps. A look at a topographical map shows a clearly defined route from the Kennebec River to Quebec, via the Carry Ponds, the Dead River, Lake Megantic and the Chaudiere River. This is the route Father Gabriel Druilletes took to visit the Norridgewock Indians in 1645. This is the same route used by General Benedict Arnold in his ill-fated attempt to capture Quebec in 1775.

Diaries written by some of Arnold's men, notably Dr. Isaac Senter, comment on the plethora of trout in the ponds encountered just west of the Carrying Place on the Kennebec River. These later became known, reading from left to right in journalistic custom, as West Carry, Middle Carry and East Carry Ponds. Whether Indians, in traveling this established route, ever strayed north to Pierce Pond, is not known, but it is well verified that the white man did.

From Justin H. Smith's *Arnold's March from Cambridge to Quebec*, we learn that the trail from the Kennebec to East Carry Pond was kept open by the sons of Seth Adams (1797-1882) as they made a business of selling trout taken from that pond. Their success soon led to the building of a fishing camp there known as Arnold Camp. Guides and fishermen being a curious lot, exploration became inevitable, especially since a highway of sorts to the north was available.

That the Indians did little fishing at Pierce Pond is evident and logical. Few artifacts have been found and there was no reason for them to go out of their way for fish. The Kennebec was so filled with salmon, shad, alewives and smelt that at times it was almost impossible to navigate.

Abenaki Indians, of which the nomadic Kennebecs were a branch, were descended from the Red Paint People who crossed the Bering Straits from Siberia and eventually arrived in Maine about 2500 B.C. The arrowheads discovered here apparently were used for hunting moose and caribou. A perfect specimen was found only a few years back by guest Charles Metcalf on the rocky island above the camps.

Identification of Indians is a bit difficult since the names handed down to us are blemished with erroneous translations, and phonetic spellings. We know that the word Abenaki is a corruption of the Indian noun Wabunong, meaning "a place of light" or the east, and was used by the French to designate the Indians in parts of Maine and New Hampshire. We also know that Red Paint People used red clay in their burial ceremonies and it has been found in excavations in the Kennebec Valley.

Furthermore, it is likely that the Indians who wandered about the Kennebec Valley from what is now Madison northward to Moosehead Lake, were known as the Norridgewogs, a branch of the Kennebecs.

We are also told that the rapids which existed in the area of the Kennebec below the Forks discouraged the Indians from spending much time above the Carrying Place Stream. Archaeologists have found little sign of Indians from Moosehead Lake down to the Forks. The first really large Indian site, according to Warren K. Moorehead in his *Archaeology of Maine*, is at Madison where Father Rale had his Catholic mission.

Another reason for Indians to avoid large, fast rivers was that the smaller tributaries were equally productive of fish and far easier to work. Henry Rowe Schoolcraft, one-time Commissioner of Indian Affairs and life-long student of the American natives, mentions several methods of taking fish from streams. In one instance, Indians have been known to dam up a stream so that only a small waterfall remained. Under this fall was placed a net of woven branches to catch those fish descending the stream. Another successful scheme was the building of a porous dam from poles tied together. On top was a walkway. When large fish, attempting to move upstream, bumped their noses against the sunken poles, the Indians could spear them.

Spearing apparently was a favorite method for taking fish. In the winter the Indians would cut holes in the ice, lower a wooden imitation of a small fish and wait for their quarry to strike. The Indians, by covering their heads with blankets of skins, were able to see clearly into the water. The spear itself was cleverly designed. The pole used had a small crotch at the end. To each of the two projecting limbs was affixed a deer horn with a barb or barbs carved out. To each horn was attached a lanyard that in turn was fastened to the throat of the crotch. When the fish was struck, it naturally struggled and pulled the deer horns away from the pole, only to be restrained by the lanyards. Spearing had a bad effect on the salmon population over the years. The Indians found the salmon most vulnerable when they were spawning in shallow water. This trick was passed along to the whites so that by 1867, when the first Fish Commissioners made their report to the governor of the state, one of their strongest grievances concerned the slaughter of salmon by avaricious fishermen.

The river is named for the Kennebis tribe the early white settlers found in the valley. S. H. Whitney tells us in *Kennebec Valley*, 1887, that the chief sachem in the area was Bashaba, who lived on Swan Island between what is now Richmond and Dresden. Reporting to him were four lesser lights who headed the four divisions of the river. The Sagadahocks ruled that part of the river between Merrymeeting Bay and the ocean and referred to their river as Sagadahock. From Merrymeeting Bay northward to Augusta lived the Cussenockes. The Tacconets inhabited the fertile valley of the Sebasticook which joins the Kennebec at Waterville. The Norridgewogs had charge of everything above Norridgewock. From Merrymeeting Bay to Skowhegan Falls, the river was called Bashaba; between Skowhegan and Solon it was called Aruntsook and from Solon to Moosehead Lake it was called Carratunk.

We know most about the Norridgewogs because of Father Rale, a Catholic missionary, who lived among them for nearly 50 years and put some of his experiences down on paper. These manuscripts were published by the American Academy of Arts and Sciences at Boston. From them we know that the tribe left every winter for Moosehead Lake for the purpose of hunting the big game of the area; that they planted their corn in the spring and then headed for the seashore in order to have seafood until the harvest was ready. This accounts for the famous shell mounds in Damariscotta and other areas.

Since there are two sides to every story, it is to one's advantage to read *The Pioneer Days of the Catholic Church in Maine*, a reprint of articles published originally in the *Maine Catholic Historical Magazine*, as well as the numerous histories written by WASP writers. Like most wars, the eventual struggle between the Indians and the whites was as much about religion as it was about land. French priests from Canada, such as Father Rale, established missions among the Indians in an effort to convert them to Christian ways. The British, on the other hand, attempted to buy up the land of the Indians. When a sachem sold land to the British, he thought he was merely giving them the right to hunt and fish on his property. He did not recognize ownership of property because in his view the land belonged to everyone in the tribe. In the struggle for possession of what later became part of the United States, the French, who were friendly with the Indians, were able to use them as allies against the British who settled on land they assumed they owned.

The Indians were intrigued by the French and the white man's God because the French missionaries gave of themselves for the benefit of the Indian, whereas the British appeared only to be interested in the Indian lands. In this case, might turned out to be stronger than right as the British eventually were triumphant and the Kennebec Indians migrated to Canada, leaving the body of their beloved Father Rale buried at Norridgewock where he had died defending their rights.

The Pioneers

Interest in the interior of Maine began shortly after the Revolutionary War, when Massachusetts realized that it owned vast forests that could be cleared by settlers. Governor John Hancock suggested to the legislature that if the Commonwealth were to sell these lands the funds received would do much to ease the state's indebtedness. Accordingly, surveys were made, a land lottery was instituted and eventually some 300,000 acres were bid for and deeded to the lucky winners. The loneliness of the territory may be realized by the fact that the population of Maine in 1764 was put at 24,000.

Those close to the government saw the possibilities as well and General Henry Lincoln of Hingham took the trouble to investigate some of the property and was impressed. He passed the word along to friends who purchased townships, on credit, with the proviso that they settle 40 families on each township within seven years. General Henry Knox, another Revolutionary hero, also was intrigued by Maine lands. He contracted for one million acres on the Upper Kennebec and fifty-two townships east of the Penobscot at ten cents an acre, or $265,000.

The Kennebec lands are the ones in which we are interested since Pierce Pond is virtually in the center of the property. The southern tier of townships in this piece runs from Mount Abram on the west to Wellington on the east. The boundary then goes north to Moosehead Lake and west to Appleton Township. Landmarks on the north include part of the Moose River and on the west, Flagstaff Lake.

William M. Morris, who investigated the property at the behest of Theophile Casinove, Esquire, a Dutch investor, had this to say about the Million Acres:

"Upon the whole I draw this general conclusion (from hunters, from my own experience, and those purposely employed to view it), that two fifths is land fit for settlement, consisting of intervale and such soil as may be improved to advantage, three fifths unsettleable consisting of mountains, sunken lands and water, besides the range of mountains continuing a course nearly N. E. and S. W. . . . . .

"No country can be said to be more healthy, of putrid and inflammatory fevers they have scarcely an instance, the diseases among children are few, and a great proportion of births are raised, the women are strong and prolific."

General Knox did not hold his property long for he inherited other Maine lands from the Waldo family into which he had married and so he looked for relief from William Bingham, a prominent Philadelphia banker. Bingham took over the Knox contract with the Commonwealth of Massachusetts and paid 12 1/2 cents per acre, or $311,250, at last in coin of the realm.

Actually it all was not as simple as that. To be thoroughly bewildered one should read *William Bingham's Maine Lands*, a hefty two-volume treatise of some 2,400 pages on the subject put out by the Colonial Society of Massachusetts in 1954.

A number of Bostonians got into the act and thereby influenced future atlases of Maine with names such as Warren, Phillips, Lowell, Otis and King. We know that Harrison Gray Otis obtained the township of Concord and the Eastern half of Lexington, and started a road to Canada, at a cost of $3,000. As early as 1810 the General Court of the Commonwealth of Massachusetts had determined that the Kennebec settlements should be connected to those on the Chaudiere River in Quebec and accordingly had proposed a road four rods wide be established. To propose is one thing; to construct is another. Dean Marriner in *Kennebec Yesterdays,* quotes William Allen of Norridgewock that it usually took 20 years from the time the first trail was blazed until it was suitable for carriages. He stated that it took two days to blaze a mile of trail, four days to widen it for pack horses and six days to make it passable for carts.

The road started by Harrison Gray Otis ran from Concord north by East Carry Pond to near the outlet of Pierce Pond, past the two Otter Ponds and across the Dead River about two miles west of The Forks. Improvements became possible in 1827 when the Maine Legislature sold Tomhegan Township for $5,485 and applied that sum to the Canada Road. A county map of 1883 shows the road clearly, but it no longer goes through to the Dead River, no doubt because the road on the east bank of the Kennebec was easier to travel and maintain.

Mr. Bingham had international stature and eventually got the Baring Brothers Company, a multi-national operation, interested in his Maine lands. The Barings sent the young Alexander over to this country to investigate the situation and in the process he met William Bingham's daughter Anna Louise, whom he married in 1798. In short order he fell heir to the Bingham lands and later appointed General David Cobb, an *aide-de-camp* of George Washington, to handle the matter of settling the estate with the Commonwealth of Massachusetts.

William Bingham had gone to London in 1802 on the recommendation of his son-in-law, Alexander Baring, and appointed one John Black, an accountant, to serve as clerk for the several agents selling the Bingham lands. Black, although only 21 years of age, did not lack for ability and sagacity. For starters he married a daughter of General Cobb. He also arranged to take all the lumber he could saw at his mills at Ellsworth without compensation. The proprietors were bent on opening up the territory for purposes of settlement and agriculture. Black saw the value in the standing timber.

It was several decades before there was any kind of land boom. In fact, the Commonwealth of Massachusetts and, after 1820, the State of Maine, gave away numerous townships in an effort to get things started. By offering townships to educational and other institutions, the legislatures killed two birds with one gift. They made some of their constituents happy and at the same time passed the buck of responsibility for the lands.

An 1829 map of the state, prepared by Moses Greenleaf, shows a patchwork quilt of townships, many of them deeded to institutions. Bowdoin College at Brunswick was, by far, the favorite, being granted the townships of Dixmont, Elna, Abbot, Guilford, Foxcroft and Sebec, plus two unnamed townships near Moosehead Lake. No doubt the shadow of James

Bowdoin, for whom the college was named, and who became governor of Massachusetts in 1785, had considerable influence. Colby, then Waterville College, received but one township, as did Williams and a host of academies. Hebron and Monson Academies divided one township while Berwick, Taunton, Fryeburgh (sic), Marblehead, Bridgton, Warren, Saco, Hopkins, Sandwich and Bath Academies each received a full township. The Maine Medical Society was honored and the townships of Freeman and New Portland were awarded to the "sufferers of Falmouth". This reference is to the burning of what is now Portland by the British in 1775.

In 1828 the timber land was run out into townships and offered at auction for a minimum of 75 cents an acre. Only two townships were sold that first day at 75 and 76 cents per acre, but the very next day one of them was resold at a dollar per acre. That started a boom which did not end until all of the timberland was sold, some of it for as much as ten dollars an acre.

William Allen, who worked for John Black for 27 years, told of his experiences in an article prepared for *The Maine Historical Society Proceedings* in 1888 and stated that after 42 years the Bingham estate was eventually compensated for the original cost of the investment plus interest on that investment, plus all moneys paid for taxes, improvements and agencies, as well as John Black's fees for services. One can understand that he was able to live well at Ellsworth in a mansion that today bears his name and is being preserved as an historic landmark.

An interesting sidebar on the Knox-Bingham-Baring business is that Alexander Baring later became Lord Ashburton and was the British representative in what became the Webster-

Ashburton Treaty that settled the boundary line between the United States and Canada.

One of the men who surveyed the Bingham lands was Eleaser Coburn, whose name graces Coburn Gore and whose son, Abner, later became governor of Maine (1863-1864). Together with Abner and another son, Philander, Eleaser spent months in the woods laying out township boundaries and the trio became as familiar with the Bingham Kennebec lands as anyone. In fact, a map of the area drawn in the 1830's shows that Eleaser, in various combinations with his sons and others, had acquired considerable property. For example, the Carrying Place Township, just south of Pierce Pond, was deeded to E. A. P. Coburn, whereas Abner Coburn had his name on Township 2, Range 2 (now Mayfield) by himself. East Moxie township was claimed by Coburns and others in combination. The Coburns eventually owned 700 square miles of timberland. Abner Coburn missed few opportunities and became president of a railroad and a bank as well as Chairman of the Board of what later became Colby College. That he was a bachelor may have helped.

Abner Coburn was not only a successful man, but a generous one as well. His will distributed more than one million dollars in cash and land to 17 institutions and organizations, including the Maine Insane Hospital, the Maine General Hospital, the Maine State College of Agriculture (later the University of Maine), Colby University (now Colby College), American Baptist Home Mission Society, the Wayland Seminary (Washington, D.C.), American Baptist Missionary Union, Maine Baptist Convention, Waterville Classical Institute (later Coburn

Classical), Houlton Academy, Maine Industrial School for Girls, Skowhegan Baptist Church, Bloomfield Academy, the town of Skowhegan, the Skowhegan Hall Association and numerous individuals. The residue was left to his nephews and nieces.

The Coburns came from a solid lineage. Abner Coburn's great grandfather, Joseph Weston, was one of the first settlers of Somerset County, having moved there from Massachusetts in 1772. He gave his life in the Revolutionary cause when he died of exposure while guiding Benedict Arnold's forces through the wilderness enroute to Quebec.

In surveying Pierce Pond Township, the Coburns divided it three ways. First, the eastern half of the township, which covers the area of Pierce Pond and environs, was separated by a line running from what is now the southern road into the pond to the Dead River. The western half of the township was split by an east-west line into the Basin Tract to the north and the Black Brook Tract to the south. The reason for this division may be that the Black Brook Tract drains in a westerly direction into the Dead River and the Basin Tract drains in a northerly direction into the same river, whereas Pierce Pond drains in an easterly direction to the Kennebec. The timber thereon could be got to water more readily. An 1820 map of the area indicates little timber on the eastern half of the township. In those days pulp wood was not a consideration.

The map of the 1830's also shows that the eastern half of the Pierce Pond Township had by then been deeded to a David Webster from Fryeburg, who paid $2,500 for the land in 1833.

Thereafter the property was tossed around like a hot potato:

1835 Webster to Martin Gore of Portland, $16,068

1837 Gore to John How of Portland, $24,000

1840 How to Charles Rogers of Portland, $12,050. This maneuver needs an explanation. There is little doubt that How took off considerable timber in the three years he owned the property. We know as well that one John Lindsay was How's agent and had charge of lumbering off the big pines around the cove that bears his name. We also know that the land boom of the 1830's fizzled out in the 1840's. Finally, any property that had been shorn of its timber was nowhere near as attractive as a stand of virgin pine.

1845 Rogers to Asa Redington of Lewiston, $3,600. This deal also included rights to the Emerson Dam sluice on Pierce Pond Stream.

1864 Redington to Charles Drummond of Winslow, $6,345.

1869 Drummond to Edward Lawrence of Fairfield, $10,000.

1880 Lawrence to Ezra and Calvin Totman, $6,000.

1891 Totman to Manufacturers Investment Company, which owned the first paper mill at Madison.

The owners and operators of the first paper mill at Madison were also among the fishermen who were responsible for discovering and developing Pierce Pond as prime salmon and trout water. They tried to keep their newly found play yard a secret, but they struggled in vain against human nature—the urge of successful fishermen to brag.

The Mystery of Pierce Pond Salmon

It has taken a full century for the story to unfold of how Pierce Pond changed from one in which eels and pickerel dominated to a home for large and succulent, if reluctant, trout and landlocked salmon. *Piscis de resistance*, one might say.

For years all that was known was that pickerel were introduced into the Dead River around 1855 and that somewhere in that period some were dropped into Pierce Pond. It was also known that eels used to work their way up Pierce Pond Stream before the Wyman Dam, built in 1930 on the Kennebec River, stopped that natural course of events. Then suddenly, a man by name of Miller from Caratunk came to Pierce Pond one day in search of pickerel and went home with an 18-pound salmon. Armond Spalding, son of the founder of Pierce Pond Camps, confirmed the story, but failed to provide a date or the scales on which the fish was weighed.

Arthur R. Macdougall, Jr., creator of *Dud Dean, Maine Guide*, ardent fly fisherman, and Bingham minister noted for his opening day services for trout fishermen, enshrined the story in prose and published it as *Crazy Stiller Goes-A-Fishing*. How salmon got into Pierce Pond was a mystery for years until Gary Cobb spent one winter digging into the file of the *Maine Woods*, a weekly printed at Phillips in the early 1900's, and the East Carry Pond Camp register. He also talked with Macdougall's grandson, Arthur Dingley, and Nellie Macdougall Parks, the Reverend's daughter.

For a proper insight, one must realize that at the turn of the century, the industrial revolution was at its height, millionaires were advertising their success by building palatial homes and proving that they could do most anything they wanted. Many of these successful men took to the woods for recreation, led by Theodore "That's Just Bully" Roosevelt. Fishing and big game hunting were attacked with the same vigor that had led to success in business. Every nimrod and angler was out to prove himself superior to his neighbor. To succeed at fishing one had to know where the big fish were and to learn that one had to hire a guide or stock his own pond!

The state and federal governments got the virus. They realized that money spent to propagate fish brought handsome returns. Accordingly hatcheries were established and stocking was done on a gigantic scale. The federal government even had special railroad cars designed and built for transporting fish eggs and fingerlings. They were capable of carrying from 25,000 to 37,500 fish at one time, depending on the size.

Thus, in 1891, a group of New York financiers bought 12,578 acres of Pierce Pond property from the Totmans under the guise of the Manufacturing Investment Company. The idea was to build a pulp mill at Madison and supply it with wood from their own property. The principal backers were William

C. Whitney, a former Secretary of the U.S. Navy, and his brother-in-law, Colonel Oliver Hazard Payne, who was also Treasurer of the Standard Oil Company. President Grover Cleveland, then between terms in office, was also said to be involved. Whitney had been a member of Cleveland's first cabinet.

It is not surprising, therefore, to find that Captain Casper F. Goodrich was given leave of absence from the Navy to supervise building the new mill at Madison. He was also interested in fishing and is directly associated with Pierce Pond salmon. Also involved was C. S. Humphreys, a civil engineer and surveyor who came to Madison in the late 1880's and became manager of the mill in 1893. Other conspirators included E. A. Merrimen, a surveyor and timber scaler who was a close friend and neighbor of Humphreys, and Frank Briggs of Pittsfield, a wool manufacturer who also had interests at Madison. His mill at Madison shared water power with the Manufacturing Investment pulp mill. A Dr. C. E. Williams of Auburn can also be cited as an accessory. These sports took advantage of the generous supply of game at Pierce Pond as well.

The East Carry Pond Camp register reveals that in 1905-06 Frank Briggs built two camps at East Carry Pond and these became known as the Kennebec Valley Club camps. The register shows that Goodrich, Humphreys, Merriman, Williams and Briggs made frequent trips to the area. In addition, the Manufacturers Investment Company did considerable cutting on its Pierce Pond property at this time, thereby offering many opportunities for ardent fishermen to traverse the area.

While newspaper copy is suspect as *prima facie* evidence, an article in the September 25, 1905 edition of the *Maine Woods*, states that a group of men from Madison was responsible for stocking Pierce Pond with salmon. That it was done *sub rosa* was to be expected, for sharing one's knowledge of such valuable information was not a custom then any more than it is today. Logic suggests that Snow and his group probably were the first to stock Pierce Pond for two good reasons. One, they were at Otter Pond in 1894, considerably ahead of Frank Briggs and his Kennebec Valley Club. Two, getting salmon fry into Pierce Pond via the Otter ponds was considerably easier than over the tortuous route that led to Pierce Pond from the tote road along Pierce Pond Stream.

But the Kennebec Valleyers had clout and it well could be that they were responsible for the U. S. Fish Commission putting 3,500 landlocked salmon into Pierce Pond in 1900 as well as a direct shipment of Quinnat salmon from the West Coast to Pierce Pond in 1904, the year they put a cabin on the pond.

Enter the Macdougall Clan. In interviewing Arthur Dingley, the Reverend's grandson, Gary Cobb learned that Jack (Dad) Owens, a close neighbor of the Macdougall's, helped to carry the first salmon fry to Pierce Pond. Dingley spent considerable time with his grandfather in Macdougall's later years and heard a number of stories about fishing in the Upper Kennebec, some that had been printed and some that had not. Owens was a guide and the source of many of the stories Macdougall wrote and published. The bit about the stocking of Pierce Pond was one that was not published because Owens had been pledged to secrecy. There is more about Owens in *The Guides* chapter, but for now it is sufficient to know that he was active in the area and part of the Pierce Pond conspiracy.

It is logical to suspect that William B. Snow, who owned Bowtown in which the Otter Ponds are located, and who was a rabid fisherman, would do something about stocking his ponds. It also makes sense that Snow, who headed the Pierce Pond Fish and Game Association, would want to stock Pierce Pond even as he was stocking the Otters. Furthermore, once one had fry as far as the Otter Ponds it was a simple matter to change water and transport them to Pierce Pond.

According to Dingley, four years later, or 1898, Owens took a party into Pierce Pond and large salmon were caught. Whether they were so big as to necessitate shooting may be another story. In fact, Dingley says his grandfather had shown him a picture of several large salmon with bullet holes in their heads and that was the basis of another of the stories that Macdougall published.

Alice Bean Kennedy Giradin, whose maiden name Bean causes heads to nod when mentioned along the Upper Kennebec, confirms the tales about shooting fish. Her husband Archie once got so frustrated at seeing big fish rise at Kilgore Pond, that he tried, without success, to kill them with a pistol.

Whether or not these stockers knew what they were doing, and Jack Owens doubted that the fry he carried over would survive, it matters not because by introducing salmon into Pierce Pond, the pickerel problem was solved. In nature's scheme of things, salmon are mightier than pickerel and so the latter became food for the newcomers who fattened rapidly.

For approximately 100 years salmon have held sway

except for two decades in the late 1950's, 1960's and early 1970's when eager biologists began stocking fingerling salmon in the fall. It turned out that these choice morsels were being fed to a horde of pickerel who promptly began making a comeback. It was not until 1980 that someone saw the light and stocked yearling fish instead. They were large enough to fend for themselves and in time salmon reigned supreme again. Today less than a dozen pickerel are caught each year.

An interesting angle on the secret stocking of Pierce Pond is the fact that H. W. Rowe, editor of the *Maine Sportsman*, published at Bangor at the turn of the century, heard the rumor about Quinnat salmon in Pierce Pond as well as one saying that the fish were steelhead trout. His source was a businessman whom he met on a train. The businessman pointed the finger at now Rear Admiral Goodrich. Accordingly Editor Rowe wrote to Goodrich, then Commander-in-Chief of the U. S. Pacific Squadron.

The admiral, who did not get to his high station without benefit of diplomacy, replied:

"I am very sorry that a regard for the truth (or, possibly, a faulty memory) makes me disclaim, with great reluctance, the honor of having planted the steelhead trout in Pierce Pond."

He did admit of having had an interest in such things and it is quite possible that he felt justified in avoiding the question since it was Quinnat salmon and not steelhead trout that were planted.

Mr. William J. Epting, a Philadelphia sportsman, wrote in the *Maine Woods* that in 1904, Frank J. Durgin, a warden and guide in the Pierce Pond area, had received by messenger and train from the Pacific Coast a lot of Quinnat fry and deposited it in Pierce Pond. Two years later Mr. Epting stopped at Pierce Pond and received three such salmon from Charles A. Spalding, operator of the camps at that time. They had been caught by Dr. W. H. Barrett of New York City, an acclaimed expert on Pierce Pond salmon, and J. W. Rafter of Gardiner, Maine, a certified member of the Kennebec Valley Club. Epting sent off the skins and anal fins to Washington for identification and received confirmation from both the Academy of Science and the Smithsonian that indeed the fish were Quinnat salmon.

In 1907 Mr. Epting, writing under the *nom de plume* of "Old Sport", reported on some of the catches at Pierce Pond, including landlocked salmon, trout and Quinnat salmon. There were 37 salmon caught, of which four were Quinnat, plus 37 trout. The Quinnat salmon all weighed 2 1/2 pounds while the landlocks ranged from three pounds to eleven. The trout scaled in at 1 1/2 pounds to six. Among the fishermen and hunters recorded were a number of members of the Kennebec Valley Club, including John O'Day, whose name once graced what is now Horseshoe Pond; Frank Briggs; F. H. Talcott of Lexington, MA; Dr. E. C. Williams; and C. S. Humphreys.

In the early days of Fish Commissions, it was assumed that the disruptions of nature had left sea salmon stranded in certain ponds and lakes. By 1900, however, W. C. Kendall of the U. S. Fish Commission stated that that theory had been found faulty and proposed that the salt water and fresh water fish were different species with the salt water variety being considered the parent.

Originally, landlocked salmon were known as Sebago

Trout and in 1867, when it made its first report, the Maine Fish Commission refused to commit itself as to the exact origin of the species. It did state that the Sebago fish as well as those caught in the Schoodic waters of Grand Lake were thought to be varieties of the sea salmon which had lost their instinct to return to the ocean. The Sebago species, once discovered, was quickly decimated and almost eliminated by avaricious fishermen using flares and spears on spawning beds.

Augustus C. Hamlin, M.D., writing in 1903, quoted an Indian guide to the effect that landlocked salmon were sea salmon who "forgot to go to sea." Hamlin was a Bowdoin graduate and a nephew of Lincoln's Vice President, Hannibal Hamlin. He served as a surgeon in the Civil War, and as a practicing physician at Bangor for 50 years. He was an ardent fisherman, even in his undergraduate days, and made a life-long study of trout and salmon. He even brought the Maine species of salmon to the attention of Professor Louis Agassiz of Harvard. That famous scientist proclaimed it to be the sea salmon, *salmo salar*.

It is entirely possible that the good professor was correct, for Hamlin reported to the U. S. Fish Commission in 1872 that in his conversations with Indian guides he (and they) had become convinced that the landlocked salmon was created when dams were erected at Sebago Lake in 1772 and at Schoodic in 1832. According to Hamlin the Indians had told him that the disappearance of sea run salmon from the Sebago and Schoodic areas coincided with the appearance of landlocked salmon there. It is no coincidence that the State of Maine, in its eagerness to provide more sport for visitors to the state, sought to increase production of these "shiners," or Sebago trout, so that other waters in the state might benefit. Eventually the state was successful and landlocked salmon became as attractive a lure for sportsmen as its famous cousin the Eastern Brook Trout or *salvelinus fontinalis.*

Anyone wishing to know more about the "good old days" of landlocked salmon fishing should look up Hamlin's article in the *Maine Sportsman* of June, 1903. Hamlin wrote about having as many as a dozen salmon leap for his fly when he cast it on Grand Lake Stream. His guide on his first trip suggested that he stop fishing after successfully landing fish on his first 25 casts as they then had more fish than they could carry.

There is no question as to the popularity of landlocked salmon throughout Maine. As early as 1867 the state attempted to hatch eggs of the Sebago variety for the purpose of meeting a growing demand. By 1891 it had solved most of the problems of planting such fish, just in time to try to satisfy the crush of fishermen being lured to Maine by those who knew what a good thing they had.

Railroads, of which there was a plethora in Maine at the turn of the century, some as short as the 15 miles from Strong to Kingfield, had as much to do with the popularity of Maine fishing as they did with lumber. In fact, the hey-days of the lumbering and sporting industries came jointly for as the railroads moved deeper into the Maine woods, they came nearer the ponds, streams and lakes that held the prized game and game fish. Maine natives, quick to smell a dollar, built fishing and hunting camps, and used advertisements to lure the city dwellers north. The railroads were equally aggressive.

The Bangor and Aroostock Railway even went so far as to publish an annual volume of information about camps, guides, record catches and trophies, time tables and even stagecoach schedules for the convenience of nimrods and fishermen. For the fisher*ma'ams* there was advice on what to wear in the north country.

The reputation of Pierce Pond salmon was aided in 1904 when the Maine Fish Commission illustrated its annual report with a picture of a 12-pound salmon taken from the pond. The *Maine Sportsman* did much to advertise the sports of fishing and hunting and seemed to have a special interest in the catches taken from Pierce Pond. Rance Ham, the Moscow guide, is mentioned on several occasions as are the camps at East Carry Pond.

It takes little imagination to realize that in due course someone was going to put a fishing camp on Pierce Pond. It is quite possible that Henry Lane, for whom Rance Ham worked, was that first person. At any rate we do know that eventually Lane put a camp on Pierce Pond as well as a man to take care of guests there. A letter written in 1903 by Rance Ham's wife, Marcia, speaks of the 16-pound whopper that Rance had taken out of Pierce Pond and of the camps that would be built there "very soon." Incidentally, any 16-pound salmon taken from Pierce Pond in 1903 had to have been stocked no later than 1895, according to one guide.

Rance Ham's 16-pounder is the closest thing to an official record for Pierce Pond, but there are two unofficial claimants to the title. (The world record is 22 1/2 pounds, taken from Sebago Lake in 1907.) One is Al Nugent who came from The

Forks and guided at Pierce Pond in the 30's before he went on to greater fame as operator of Nugent's Camps on Chamberlain Lake. One day he had a party down near the outlet and noticed a big fish that had been caught in a sluice gate. Al was all for taking it back to camp, but one member of his party was stricken with compassion and persuaded the guide to let the fish have its liberty. Nugent judged the fish to have weighed 18 pounds, and to be three and a quarter feet in length, or half of his 6-foot, 6-inch paddle.

The other claimant is one Anthony Comber, a logger, who said he caught an 18 to 20-pounder while fishing from a raft near the Grass Pond landing. Comber's grandson, who lives at Pleasant Pond, remembers the fish, but *how* well may be described by the poem that starts:

"Two pounds was the fish when he came from the lake
And three when they got him ashore.
By night he weighed five; and the very next day,
They added a pound or two more."

Such sockdolagers, unfortunately, are history, for in later years the top salmon have been of more modest proportions. Between 1957 when Perry Grieve established the custom of recording prize fish on boards at the camps, and the present, the biggest salmon taken were seven pounds, seven ounces each. They were caught by Clare Bousquet of Pittsfield, Massachusetts in 1963 and by Bob Rice, another Bay Stater, from Barre in 1964.

Lumbering

From the early days of the white man in America, fishing, hunting and lumbering went hand in hand in the Maine woods. They still do, though not as cozily as they once did. The early settlers of Maine worked their way up the rivers, cutting and clearing the banks. From the trees came the material for their log cabins and from the rivers and the adjacent woods came the fish and game that formed the basis of their diet.

To give some perspective to the history of lumbering in Maine, one should know that the first saw mill in the state is said to have been established at Kennebunk in 1623. By 1650 Boston had become a leading port for the shipment of lumber to the Caribbean. Thereafter, until after the Revolutionary War, pine was the most wanted product. England, with its large merchant and naval fleets, desperately needed the large white pines for masts and much of her foreign policy was plotted with *pinus strobus* in mind. Once the war was over, land in Maine was considered an asset to be used as a means of paying off the victorious rebel army and as collateral for loans to defray the national debt. The vast forests on this land were not a major consideration in the beginning of the new republic. The main objective was to people the wilderness with pioneers who eventually would become landowners and taxpayers.

It was not long before the wealth of resources in the new country became the target of commercial activity on the part of both England and the colonists. The colonists were unhappy to have what they saw as their property being appropriated by the Crown. Subterfuge attacked the dictum from London that all white pine trees more than 24 inches in diameter should be reserved for the Royal Navy. The colonists wanted these trees as much for their own merchant fleet as for the lumber involved. For the most part they got what they wanted, even if they did have to reduce some boards to 23 inches in width in order to make certain they were not confiscated.

The search for white pine reached the Pierce Pond area in 1832 when Myrick and Jacob Emerson of Orono constructed a dam and a sluiceway at the outlet. The next year a contract was drawn between them and a John Grover, stating that "Emerson shall sluice and drive to Waterville all lumber cut and hauled on the east half of T2R4, Pierce Pond." Grover agreed to pay 1 1/2 cents per thousand feet board measure for the privilege of using the Emerson facility. A year later, as one might expect, the State Legislature granted a charter to the Emersons.

These documents, now in the State Archives and the Somerset County Registry, are important for several reasons. First, they mark the first time that Pierce Pond was given a name. It came about casually. Nathaniel Pierce, the grandson of an early Norridgewock settler and himself a native of Bingham, served in the War of 1812 and for his service he was granted land for a homestead. He settled on the north bank of Pierce's Stream on the Kennebec River. He married Adra Baker of The Forks, who bore him nine children, including Osborne who eventually inherited the property.

Nathaniel is believed to have done surveying in Bowtown and Pierce Pond and obviously was of sound stock as he lived to be 92 years of age. He survived his wife by 10 years and then was buried beside her in the Caratunk Cemetery. A map of the area drawn in 1850 shows the names of the families which had settled along both sides of the Kennebec River including, in addition to the Pierces, the Spaldings, Adams, Sanborns, Collins, Browns and Gilroys. All that remains on the west side of the river are cellar holes overgrown with poplar and birch.

The Emerson Dam may be the first dam chartered by the State. As has been said, the lumbering era was just beginning at this time and tote roads were being hacked out of the forest, such as the one that used to run from Lindsay Cove to the dam. At this time, men such as John Grover were buying "stumpage", or standing timber, which they cut and twitched and floated down stream to the waiting saw mills.

A second distinction of the Emerson Dam was that its charter was the first to give the right to charge a toll for logs passing through it. To avoid confusion down stream, each log carried the trademark of its owner, just as old Eleaser Coburn used to mark the cedar posts he placed at the boundaries on the townships and lots he surveyed. Each surveyor and lumberman had his own distinctive sign, or brand, just as cattlemen did out west.

Many factors contributed to the record harvests of the

Maine woods. The state had the perfect climate for the primitive means of the 19th century for moving logs from woodland to saw mill. Severe winters brought lots of snow which aided oxen in twitching and skidding logs to the shore of pond and river. Spring freshets raised water levels so the logs might be floated down streams to rivers and thence to saw mills powered by these same rivers. Farmers welcomed a chance to earn some cash during the off season, even though the wages of men in the woods were only $12 to $20 per month, plus food, for six days per week from 5 a.m. to dark.

That Pierce Pond was thoroughly denuded of its great pines is attested by the many logging sites found in the area. No doubt Lindsay Cove saw the first one as oxen shoes were found there by Bob Estes, former woods boss for Great Northern Paper Company, in the early 1950's. Other sites include the present camp grounds which, according to a newspaper account in 1947, were part of the pulp land acquired by the Manufacturing Investment Company for its mill at Madison.

It is also significant that the former lumber camps make ideal spots for guides to have cookouts for their guests. Examples include one to the east of the Thoroughfare which leads into Upper Pierce Pond, another at the old Grass Pond landing near the back channel in the Upper Pond; a third on Dixon Brook; a fourth on Horseshoe Pond, where Gary Cobb found a three-legged iron kettle in the cooking pit of the camp; and a fifth on Pierce Mountain. All of these camps sent their logs down stream to Pierce Pond whence they were kedged by "head-works" across the pond to the outlet and thus to the Kennebec.

A headworks was a heavy raft on which a capstan was

mounted. It was used to move booms of logs to the outlet. It was operated by putting an anchor into a boat and moving it out in the direction desired and then dropping it. The line from the anchor was then wrapped around the capstan of the head-works which was manned by a crew of eight or so men. By taking up on the line the headworks and the attached boom were inched across the pond. This process was repeated until the boom was at the outlet. There is still a headworks and capstan rotting on the western shore forming the Basin.

Logging camps required tote roads which served fisher-men as well as loggers. There is no question that the three-mile trail from the Kennebec River to the outlet of Pierce Pond was used by fishermen as was the old road from the dam to Lindsay Cove. These were the only passageways available to fishermen from the 1890's to 1952 and they were also used by the Appa-lachian Mountain Club until 1950 when Flagstaff Lake was formed by the damming of the Dead River. The Trail still comes up from the Kennebec to the Pierce Pond dam, but now it heads south to East Carry Pond, whereas it used to head west to Basin Pond. An AMC hut is maintained near the Pierce Pond outlet.

Just as there was a sluiceway out of Pierce Pond, so too there were many on the lower Dead River. The section of the river north of Pierce Pond was one of the major river driving routes. That stretch of river is one of the most rugged in the state and every three miles there are still signs of sluices, usually about 300 yards long, heading right into the river. Back from each sluice is an old tote road heading into the forest, and beside each sluice, a river driving camp. Two such camps still bear their old names, "Hayden's Landing" and "Appletree Inn."

The logging camp of the mid-1800's was very crude. A temporary one-story building was thrown up around an open cooking pit, made of logs and filled with sand. There was an opening in the roof through which the smoke was supposed to flow. It rarely did. Most of the cooking was done in a single kettle and the men slept in one common bunk.

After the pine was cut during the mid-1800's, the forest around Pierce Pond was idle until the loggers returned in the 1890's to get the spruce that reposed in the higher altitudes. The oxen were replaced by horses and the camps were improved with the addition of wood stoves for heating and cooking. The men still shared common bunks, holding as many as six men. Methods of logging were much the same although the Lombard, a steam driven tractor-like contraption, enabled the loggers to haul greater quantities of logs out of the backwoods. Cutting was still more selective than today's clear-cutting practices. The narrow "twitch trails" used by horses were easier on the forest and game and did not cause the erosion that comes from eliminating all growth on a given section of timber.

From a business point of view, clear-cutting hardwoods and replanting with faster growing softwoods, makes sense and cents. So far those areas that have been cut around Pierce Pond cannot be seen from the pond. Until very recently, the hardwoods in the township were of virgin growth, but advances in technology have enabled mills to use the harder varieties in making pulp paper.

The founders of the new country had come from the leading sea power in the world, had crossed the Atlantic by boat and were aware that such organizations as the East India

Company were very profitable operations. It was instinctive that they should look to the sea for survival. Shipbuilding began early. The Popham Colony, for example, situated at the mouth of the Kennebec, launched the *Virginia* in 1608. Furthermore, since there were few respectable roads in New England, most people traveled by boat from coastal or river town. With those who wanted to build houses and those who wanted to build ships, the demand for timber grew at a steady pace. The height of the lumber industry came between 1820, when Maine became a state, and 1861, the beginning of the Civil War.

The railroads also had reached the deep woods by this time and helped to ease the rising demand for wood and wood products. We of the Plastic Age may not realize it, but hundreds of items were once made from wood: sashes, doors, blinds, furniture, carriages, sleighs, rakes, shovels, hoe handles, bobbins, spools, boxes, barrels, boats, pails, bedsteads, spokes, hubs, excelsior, shoe pegs, coffins, tubs, kegs, oars, clothes pins, toothpicks, hoops, churns, and potash, to tick off the more obvious ones.

The demand for pine tapered off gradually and in 1850 spruce was driven down the Kennebec for the first time. By 1879 pine represented only 20% of the timber cut in Maine. It was in the mid-1850's that the saw began to replace the axe as the tool for felling trees and by 1868 the pulp paper industry had come into being.

There are still vestiges of the old lumber industry in the Pierce Pond area for those who know what to look for. Around the pond itself are huge stumps of the mammoth white pine that once rimmed these waters. Here and there on the slopes to the pond are "snubbing posts" which assisted teams of horses hauling sleds loaded with logs. A heavy rope was tied to the sled and then turned around the snubbing post to keep the horses from being given a sled ride by a runaway load. Many of the logging artifacts on display in and around the present camp dining hall and office came from the numerous lumber camp sites previously mentioned. There is also a gigantic red stump, complete with axe marks, on the trail to Kilgore Pond.

Iral Bean, who guided out of Pierce and Otter Ponds between the two World Wars, told Gary Cobb that his father had used the slope of Pierce Pond Mountain to sluice logs down to the pond. Howard Mitchell, whose family was involved with Pierce Pond Camps from 1922 to 1941, confirms the story.

Sherm Bean, Iral's father, had a lumber camp at Lindsay Cove and another at High Pond on the mountain. Gary figures that Sherm anchored some guide logs along the sluicing area and then let nature take its course. As proof he has found rotting logs at the bottom of the slide as well as a piece of rusty metal. From Armond Spalding it was also learned that around 1900, when Sherm Bean was operating, there was an especially fine stand of spruce up on the mountain in a bowl that faces south. Fifty years later Great Northern Paper Company cut spruce again in the same spot.

From 1915 to 1951 the woods around Pierce Pond were not disturbed. They grew into a magnificent forest which Great Northern Paper Company recognized as a prime source of pulpwood. In anticipation the company built the present road to the pond from the south in 1951 and erected a 60-man, 30-horse lumber camp at Lindsay Cove. The company even rebuilt the old tote road to the dam from Lindsay Cove and put a crane over that road for the purpose of rebuilding the dam and sluiceway at the outlet. Then came the Fire of 1952 and these plans were abandoned. More than 1,600 acres were burned as well as some 7,000 cords of pulp wood already stacked for shipment. The woods north of Pierce Pond were not touched until 1968 when Gus Poulin contracted to cut around the upper ponds for the Madison Pulp and Paper Company. He built most of the logging roads that led to his base at Lower Otter Pond. At the time he said that the stand of timber around Kilgore, King and Grass Ponds was the best in the state.

Over the years there was some concern for the environment. A law prohibiting the dumping of lumber refuse, particularly sawdust, into streams and rivers was passed by the Maine legislature in 1834 but there was no real method of enforcement, and the oyster beds in the Sheepscot River disappeared. Thirty years later the state of New York put a blue line on a map of the Adirondacks in an effort to preserve some 5,000,000 acres that "shall be forever wild." This is the same phrase that ex-governor Percy Baxter used when he gave the people of the State of Maine the park later named for him. In 1898 the International Paper Company hired its first forester to work on the idea of replanting the forest in order to get a sustained yield. Thanks to that forester, Austin Cary, of East Machias, the economics of sustained yields was proved. Hence, the bulk of the Maine Woods is still owned and controlled by the major wood products companies. So far these companies have been sympathetic to hunters and fishers and continue to lease properties to responsible camp operators.

Electric Power

Ever since man entered the Maine Woods he has been despoiling them one way or another. First it was dams to power the saw mills, then it was dams for easy transportation of wood to those mills. The need and the desire to wrench dollars from the natural resources took top priority. As forest products of the state went from lumber to paper, the demand for electric power increased. It was aided and abetted by the increase in population.

Pierce Pond, with its proximity to both the Dead and Kennebec Rivers, has played a part in both industries and may be called on again in the future. We have shown what happened in these parts while the timber was being harvested, but we did not point out that Pierce Pond Township has had a rather checkered career as both the paper and power companies schemed and maneuvered.

As far back as 1822 the Dead River Company was formed to facilitate log drives on the Kennebec River. It was owned by landowners along the Dead River and consisted of 600 feet of dams and locks for the purpose of controlling the flow of water and hence, logs. One hundred and one years later the Kennebec Reservoir Company was formed to expand the holding capacity on the Dead River. It had been determined for many years that Long Falls was the ideal spot for a dam on the Kennebec's largest contributary. However, at that precise spot the state still owned a small amount of land and undeveloped water power and legislation to get control of these became a chapter in what continues to be a long and bitter struggle between private enterprise and those advocating state control of rivers, water power and natural resources.

The original bill creating the Kennebec Reservoir Company was passed in 1923 over the veto of Governor Baxter, who then went to the legislature personally, calling for a repeal and offering a bill of his own which would include a long term lease, rather than an outright grant to the new company. This was adopted, but after Baxter left office in 1925, the lease period was extended.

The viability of Pierce Pond as trout and salmon water was threatened in 1938 when the federal government, still anxious to find public works projects that would alleviate the depression, sent the Army Corps of Engineers to study the Dead River north of Pierce Pond, as well as the pond itself, for flood control. The scheme, as outlined in the *Somerset County Press* of Bingham on November 4, called for raising the Dead River 25 feet so as to flood the area from Long Falls to Bog Brook, west of Pierce Pond. This would place the water five feet above the level of Pierce Pond itself. A flume would be created to connect the river with the pond and another flume would connect Pierce Pond with the Kennebec through Pierce Pond Stream.

To help pay for the project a 42,000-kilowatt power station would be placed on the Kennebec at the mouth of Pierce Pond Stream. In addition, loggers would be able to avoid 16 miles of tortuous rapids and bends in the river between Long Falls and The Forks. Presumably the river would become dry in that area, except for the small streams that empty into it. Fortunately for Pierce Pond, World War II was in the making and the U. S. Army and U. S. Government soon had more important matters to consider.

It was not until 1950 that there was action on the Kennebec River Reservoir Company legislation. A huge reservoir dam was created, flooding Flagstaff Pond and the Dead River all the way back to Stratton. Great Northern Paper Company contributed $100,000 to the cost of this dam, which can impound some 12 billion cubic feet of water.

In creating Flagstaff Lake the town of Flagstaff, named for the site of the one placed there by General Benedict Arnold on his trek to Quebec, was submerged after 150 years of existence. It did not happen overnight. Central Maine Power Company bought its first house in Flagstaff in 1918 and continued to buy up properties, using some outlying farms as camps for harvesting timber, and allowing others to disintegrate. When completed 32 years later the lake extended for 24 miles, was three miles wide and encompassed 24,000 acres.

Pierce Pond almost got into the pulpwood business in 1951 when Great Northern Paper Company began implementing a plan to harvest at the southern end of the pond. Fortunately, the fire of 1952 put an end to that venture and forced Great Northern Paper Company to change its commitments. In 1954 it decided it no longer wanted to be bothered with the pulp mill at Madison, so offered it, together with a large amount of woodland to Hollingsworth and Whitney. Scott Paper Company, taking over Hollingsworth and Whitney, was interested in the woodlands, but not the mill, so it sold the mill to Economy Corporation, a holding company owned by Louis Calder. When transactions were finally concluded, Scott Paper Company owned Pierce Pond, and pieces of Dead River, Flagstaff, Caratunk, Kingfield, Jerusalem (Carrrabasset Valley), Crockertown (the Sugarloaf Mountain area), and Mount Abram Townships.

The same year GNP transferred the rights and property of the Emerson Dam to Central Maine Power Company. Utilities are continually playing games of make believe, gazing at crystal balls and trying to conjure up the moves they might make ten years down the road. Pierce Pond Stream is tumultuous, said to drop 900 feet in three miles as it rushes to join the Kennebec. In the older days it was scarcely necessary to mark logs from Pierce Pond because they were easily distinguished when they reached the river. Most were battered and bruised and many even broken. The stream might warrant a power station one day.

In 1975 one of CMP's many studies indicated that it might make sense to pump water from the Dead River into the Pierce Pond Basin to be discharged through penstocks and turbines down rapid Pierce Pond Stream. Fortunately for Pierce Pond, Maine Yankee at Wiscasset was proving a success. Accordingly, Central Maine Power deeded Emerson Dam and the various rights and privileges thereto to Floyd Cobb, in 1976. Since then the title has been passed to Gary Cobb, who has the burden of keeping the dam in repair, not for the business of floating logs, but in order to keep big fish in the pond.

As stated above, Pierce Pond Stream is a vicious one, so much so that fish, once they have made the downward journey, are unable to get back. This fact came to light in 1953 when a spring flood took out the dam. Large fish began to be caught in the Kennebec where the stream joins the river. Floyd Cobb, who had taken over the camps from Perry Grieves in 1958, put a plug in the leak. With a crew of mostly guides, including Iral and Eldie Bean, Lester Arsenault, Alfred Marble, Ralph Griffen, Omer Richards, Gary Cobb, and Charlie Norris, Floyd attacked the job.

Iral Bean probably was looked on as the chief engineer as he took care of all of the blasting and more or less called the shots. After the site was cleared big logs were placed, cribbed and back-filled with stone. Finally, the front was faced with lumber and a screen placed at one end. Pierce Pond has plenty of water. In the logging days it was known to have a "ten foot head." That, of course, was for the original dam which was about 30 yards east of the present one.

As Gary Cobb repairs the Emerson Dam each year he must keep wondering if and when Central Maine Power Company may change its mind again and opt to send water down through the Pierce Pond Basin.

The Dams and the Damned

When European explorers began to come to these shores and write of their experiences, the dominant theme trumpeted was the abundance of game, fish and natural resources of the new land. Early in the 17th century, Richard Hakluyt (1553-1616), whose studies of early exploration fathered a research industry in Great Britain that still exists, summarized the findings of six explorers, from Verazanus to Best, by describing among other things "the rivers full of incredible store of all good fishe."

In 1602, Captain Bartholomew Gosnold discovered and named Cape Cod on the basis of the impressive number of that species to be found in the area. Seven years later Henry Hudson, finding himself at what he determined to be 44 degrees, 26 minutes of latitude, or somewhere off the Nova Scotia coast, reported that his crew caught 118 great cod in five hours of fishing. That's one every two-and-a-half minutes. Finally, Captain John Smith, writing in 1620 noted "an incredible abundance of fish," primarily cod, off the New England coast.

What all this has to do with the inland fisheries of Maine

may be seen in the statement of Professor Spencer F. Baird of the Smithsonian Institute and Chief of the U.S. Bureau of Fish and Fisheries in 1872. The Fish Commissioners of Maine had written the professor to seek an explanation for the scarcity of fish and here is his reply:

"We are very well aware that fifty or more years ago (circa 1822), the streams and rivers of New England emptying into the ocean were crowded, and almost blockaded at certain seasons, by the number of shad, salmon and alewives seeking to ascend, for the purpose of depositing their spawn, and that even after these parent fish had returned to the ocean, their progeny swarmed to an almost inconceivable extent in the same localities, and later in the year descended into the ocean in immense schools. It was during this period that the deep sea fisheries of the coast were also of great extent and value. Cod, haddock, halibut and the line fish generally, occupied the fishing grounds close to the shore and could be caught from small, open boats, ample fares being readily taken within a short distance of fishermen's abodes."

What the Fish Commissioners of Maine had not realized was that the anadromous fish of the Maine rivers were part of a food chain that supplied the larger species out in the ocean. That the cod, haddock, halibut *et al* were close to shore, was due to the plethora of bait fish that was to be had for the taking. In later years when the bait supply slackened off, the larger species of ocean fish moved off shore.

What broke the food chain was the Industrial Revolution,

the need for water power. As dams were constructed on the rivers and streams of the state, access to spawning grounds for anadromous fish was limited. As salmon, shad and alewives were stymied in their desire to propagate, their numbers gradually dwindled. The Kennebec Locks and Canal Company completed its dam at Augusta in 1837.

The State of Maine did not take any official action until 1867 when two Fish Commissioners were appointed by the governor under the "Resolve relative to the Restoration of Sea Fish to the Rivers and Inland Waters of Maine." The gentlemen, named Nathan W. Foster and Charles G. Atkins, did not report until January 16 of 1868, but when they did they had 91 pages of damming and damning information. Their conclusions as to the causes of the dearth of sea fish were threefold:

1. Impassable dams
2. Over-fishing
3. Pollution

The evidence they presented was as complete as possible, considering that they had started from scratch. They also concentrated on the Kennebec River, for want of time and possibly because Charles Atkins, who later was to graduate to the U. S. Bureau of Fish and Fisheries, lived near Augusta and appears to have been the dominant member of the Commission.

The early reports by the Maine Commissioners are exceptionally intriguing for the frustrated fishermen of today. The two men interviewed long-time residents along the Kennebec and learned that one weir in one spectacular year would net 6,000 to 7,000 shad per tide; that the towns of Bowdoinham,

Dresden and Woolwich netted 1,833 barrels of shad in 1831; that the estimated number of salmon taken at Augusta in 1820 was 4,000; that in the earlier years it was easy to load a boat with salmon at Caratunk Falls.

The reports of the Commissioners from 1867 through 1882 run to some 550 pages and cover everything one might expect, from anadromous fish, the original target, to breeding and stocking of fish, to comparisons of expenditures for similar purposes in France, England, Scotland and Holland, and speculation on the origins of the land-locked salmon. They also got into such matters as guides, the number of sporting camps and licenses. In 1972-73 the Commission looked into breeding trout that would live longer and around 1980 it introduced 1,600 splake, a cross between brook trout and lake trout, into Maine lakes.

In the beginning the Commissioners were primarily concerned with providing more fish as food, but after several years they changed their focus to providing fish for recreational purposes. Early on they realized that as the railroads stretched farther north and east into the woods, they also opened up the inland fisheries to visiting sportsmen who left money in the state. They also discovered that other states were charging fishermen and hunters a fee and that by selling licenses the state could procure monies for use in the business of providing more fish and game.

More than 100 years later the struggle between dam proponents and the fishing fraternity continues. In 1867 the Fish Commissioners stated that salmon had been extinguished in the Saco, Mousam and Cobscook Rivers. At that time the

Penobscot had no impassable dams and produced more salmon than all other rivers combined. A fishway was built at Bangor in 1877 and again in 1924. In 1971-72 the Inland Fisheries and Game Department proudly announced that a fishway at Bolster's Mills and the breaching of a dam at Scribner's Mills opened up the upper reaches of the Crooked River, a tributary of Sebago Lake, to migrating salmon for the first time in 150 years.

The situation inland, however, is considerably better. Circumstances altered the case for ponds and lakes. There were those who wished to preserve and even augment the fish therein and even the corporations which owned the woodlands had ulterior motives in leasing their lands to camp operators. They realized that it was better to have game and fish lovers operating in the woods than to leave the fate of the forests in the hands of the general public. Free access to the woods had become, in the minds of native Maineacs, something approaching a constitutional right. To take deer or trout out of season was the custom for many. This was food for the table, laws or no laws.

Accordingly a number of fishing and hunting camps have survived because land owners knew that the men and women who ran these operations cared as much for the woodlands as the owners did and would do anything possible to protect them. In essence, by leasing land to camp operators the paper companies were putting that many game and fire wardens in the woods.

The small dams that had been erected to facilitate the movement of logs to market, now served as protectors of the *status quo* of fishing in the ponds and lakes effected. Furthermore, camp operators saw to it that these dams were maintained.

The State of Maine, ever willing to do whatever would attract sports has, from 1867, attempted to maintain and increase the amount of game and fish available. Knowing that camp operators were on the side of the angels, so to speak, the State has regularly stocked those ponds under the control of the men and women who make a living from them. As for Pierce Pond, it is no longer necessary to stock trout as they seem to thrive on their own, and after nearly a century of stocking salmon, the plan now is to reduce the number of salmon to 800 every other year.

The Early Sporting Years

To get back to the beginnings of the sporting scene at Pierce Pond, one must look southward to East Carry Pond. A camp had been established there as early as 1856, no doubt because of the tales of large and numerous trout that had been bruited about ever since the Adams brothers took 1,100 pounds of *salvelinus fontinalis* from the pond in one year. In the 1870's a group calling itself The Arnold Trail Club took over the camp for its private use. It does not take much imagination to figure that the members of the Arnold Club soon must have found their way up the old Canada Road from near East Carry Pond to Pierce Pond.

There were also caribou in the area. This accounts for the name Caribou Narrows in Lower Pierce Pond. In addition, the fact that the land around Pierce Pond was owned by a corporation, Manufacturers Investment Company, which operated a paper mill at Madison, explains why Pierce Pond became a well-kept secret from the general public. Armond Spalding (born in 1894), who later operated Pierce Pond Camps as we know them today, recalls such names as Humphreys, Snow and Williams among those officials of the Investment Company who came to Pierce Pond.

It is also significant that a cook shack and dining room built in the late 1890's on a point near Lindsay Cove was made from a combination of logs, shingles, boards, and mill felt, which, in this day, would undoubtedly be charged off to business expense.

In the meantime the Spalding family of Caratunk was getting into the picture. They were pioneers of the first water, being descended from Edward Spalding, who reached the Virginia colonies in 1623. In Maine they became lumbermen, river drivers, trappers and guides. They were fertile and populated both sides of the Kennebec River and along the Canada Road. They were also early settlers of New Portland, Lexington, Highland, Flagstaff and Dead River.

Charles Spalding, of the eighth generation after Edward of Virginia, built a logging camp somewhere back of the eastern shore of Lower Pierce Pond in 1896, according to his diary, now held by his grandson, Richard Spalding of Caratunk. He also recorded the facts that he carried his provisions across the Kennebec at a point called "The Crosby Landing", brought them over a tote road to his camp, hired three men to help him, and transplanted his wife, Elmedia, and three children, Harry, Christie and Armond to the new location.

This lumber camp was operated for three seasons, and after the last log had been floated to the mill on the Kennebec, Charles recorded a balance of $500 in his account book. This was his net income for the year. He considered it a very good one.

There is a gap in the Spalding records for the years 1899 to a new career for Charles Spalding in 1904. In that year, the Great Northern Paper Company, which evolved from the Manufacturers Investment Company, became worried over the number of hunters and fishermen who had discovered the beauties and game of Pierce Pond. Accordingly, they approached Charles Spalding with the proposition that he build and operate a sporting camp to accommodate the sportsmen who were camping in the area and increasing the chance of fire. They offered him a rent-free lease.

This was the beginning of Pierce Pond Camps. The Pierce Pond Fish and Game group had gotten as far as building a modest clubhouse on the present location, having considered it more propitious than Lindsay Cove. Charles Spalding at once converted one side of this clubhouse into living quarters for his family and used the other half as a kitchen to feed the guests. Tent platforms were placed more or less where the present guest camps are located. In addition, Spalding went down to the outlet where a former lumber camp still stood, had it dismantled, the logs marked with a hot iron, hauled across the ice and rebuilt where the lilac bushes now prosper. This building served first as sleeping quarters and then as an ice house. Eventually, as with most log buildings, it was taken down.

In all, Charles Spalding built five cabins between 1904 and 1906, and as each was constructed it was filled with guests. The news of the big salmon being caught at the pond could not be suppressed. Aware of the traffic being developed, the Great Northern Paper Company in 1906 levied a $50 per year charge for the use of its land.

Charles Spalding was the right man at the right time at the right place. As a woodsman he knew timber and he knew how to use it. Besides the five buildings already mentioned, he built a guides' cabin and a cabin for the help, plus a cabin on the island due east across the pond, for the Holbrook family. With his sons Armond and Harry, he stocked all of the smaller ponds in the area. They used double pails (to provide oxygen for the trout enroute) and lugged them with the aid of yokes up the slopes, even unto High and Helen Ponds. They caught minnows in Pierce Pond as feed for the fingerlings they had planted. Two years after stocking High Pond, Charles Spalding caught a 3 1/2-pound trout there.

In addition to his talents as guide, lumberman, builder, and fisherman, Charles Spalding was also something of a writer. By way of advertising his camp he wrote an account of Benedict Arnold's trek through the area enroute to Quebec and used it to help promote his business. He was gregarious and after 13 years of sharing toasts with his libation-loving guests he deemed it wise to turn over the business to his son Armond and to go back to the woods for the Great Northern Paper Company. That was in 1916, and he lived on for another 19 years, dying in 1935. He is buried in the Bingham Village cemetery, along with his wife of 47 years, who died in 1947.

More Spaldings and Others

Charles Spalding was by no means alone in his nurturing of the Pierce Pond tradition. His son Harry and Harry's wife, Annie, worked at the pond in the early 1900's. Later, their son Richard, who still lives at Bingham, was a guide. Then there was George Spalding, a boat builder as well as a house builder. He was a cousin of Armond Spalding, the second son, who took over the camps in 1916.

Armond Spalding, as we have seen, grew up in the woods of Pierce Pond Township and was well equipped to carry on as proprietor of the camps. He could handle any of the numerous jobs confronting an operator, was an excellent guide, a handy builder, and a superlative canoeist. As a 12-year-old he caught a 5 1/2-pound trout and soon became known as the "boy" guide, as he was given a special guide's license at age sixteen. He used the old clubhouse for two years and then, with the aid of another man, constructed the present dining room and kitchen.

He also had one of the first outboard motors on the pond. It was an Evinrude which he used to bring guests the three miles from the outlet to the camp. He also had a "tote boat", a bateau powered by a Palmer inboard engine. Getting from Caratunk to the camp was no easy job, especially with supplies. To begin with there was a steep descent on the east bank of the Kennebec down which one had to go before poling a bateau across the river. Next came a three-mile trek in which the driver of the camp wagon used long reins so he could walk beside the vehicle because the trail was so rough. Finally, there were the three miles across the pond which could be treacherous at times.

In the busy season two trips were made each week for supplies, and Armond, who was a good businessman, got his canned goods from S. S. Pierce Company of Boston, since a number of his guests came from the Bean Town. S. S. Pierce supplied many U. S. Embassies around the world as well as the Brahmins of Beacon Hill. And Armond saw to it that the meat he served his guests was prime, corn-fed Western beef.

Keeping guests happy by serving good food was a ritual in most sporting camps, especially in the early years of the 20th century when a man's success was measured by his girth. These were the days of plenty in the woods when limits included 25 pounds of trout and two deer per hunter. A typical camp menu published by the Maine Central Railroad at the turn of the century included, for breakfast alone, berries, oatmeal, broiled venison steak, broiled partridge, biscuits, corn bread, griddle cakes with maple syrup and coffee. Dinner and supper were even more bountiful, offering salmon, duck, rabbit, trout, raccoon, woodcock, not to mention vegetables and dessert.

Armond Spalding carried on the stocking program that

he and his father had begun. In fact, it became a hobby with him. In order to protect his fish from eager fishermen he would change the name of the ponds that he and others stocked. For example, Little Kilgore Pond became King Pond because Warden Ed King helped Armond on one trip and High-Lo Pond became Helen Pond in honor of Helen Holbrook of Boston who was a member of the party involved in putting fish into that body of water. One has to understand that the higher ponds had no fish until the Spaldings stocked them and so successful was their enterprise that in time five-pound trout were so common that it became the custom to put back anything smaller.

Helen Holbrook and her husband, Harry, acquired their lease on what is now Abbe's Island through a combination of bad and good luck. Harry was traveling on the night train from Boston to New York when Garret Schenck, the first President of the Great Northern Paper Company, apparently choked on a particle of food, while dining. Harry Holbrook was quick to recognize the problem and to apply the pressure that dislodged the impediment. In appreciation Schenck arranged for the Holbrooks to obtain a lease on the island. The cabin was built in 1910.

Twenty-five years later, Charles Abbe, Sr. made inquiries about the island and learned that Harry Holbrook was in a nursing home. Mr. Abbe visited Mr. Holbrook and persuaded him to sell the camp. Once again, Iral Bean, who served as a caretaker over the years, had a hand in the deal. Members of the Abbe family are still the privileged occupants.

Not everyone released fish in those days. Many fish were left to spoil and had to be buried. One group of fishermen from

Belgrade brought in 250 pounds of fish, had a picture taken and then buried most of them. That picture graced the wall of a Belgrade inn for years. On another occasion a sport who was unable to walk to Dixon Pond, which produced the tastiest trout in the area, told Armond he would pay $5 for every fish Armond could bring to him. His appetite must have been fully satisfied for Armond came back with the limit, which at $5 per head cost the guest $125.

Armond was the ideal camp operator, but unfortunately his wife was not. She frequently had run-ins with guests and help, making for an intolerable situation. After five years Armond decided to throw in the sponge. William Beardsell, an ardent fly fisherman, whose granddaughter, Louise Breed Allen, still comes to Pierce Pond, did his best to get Armond to stay and was willing to put his pocket book where his mouth was, but at the time Armond could not be deterred. Later he admitted it was the greatest mistake of his life.

In 1921 the camps and lease were sold to James Kelleher, an executive of the Central Maine Power Company. It could be that he had malice aforethought because his company was then considering the possibility of a dam on the Kennebec River, an idea that he had promulgated. There was a chance that Pierce Pond might be included in the scheme and Kelleher, when it became clear that this was not to be, lost interest and sold the camps to a group from Caratunk, headed by Charles Mitchell, in June of 1922. Eight years later the Wyman Dam at Bingham was completed.

The new owners made a good combination. Mitchell was a woodsman and guide and along with his wife, Nettie, ran a good camp. He was the kind of man who could lift a barrel of flour out of a boat with ease. Albert Clark owned a store at Caratunk, was also the postmaster, and was in a position to supply the necessities. Will Whorff was the stage driver from Bingham north for 49 years and had a big house in the village that became the overnight stop for guests coming to Pierce Pond. Fred Clark was a silent partner.

Will Whorff, the stage driver, was the most famous of the group, primarily because he stuck to his trade for 50 years, from 1893, when he was 19 years old, until 1943 when he retired at age 69. He also could boast that in that time he travelled more than 600,000 miles without serious accident or injury to any passenger. For the first 15 years he drove from Bingham to the Forks, a round trip of 46 miles. Later he moved to Caratunk which cut his daily run to some 30 miles. His original stage was a heavy wagon with seats for 12 which were usually filled with lumberjacks, sportsmen or river drivers, depending on the season. On occasion a log-driving shack operated by the Kennebec Log Driving Company would be in action along the river and the camp cook would flag the stage and offer dough-nuts and coffee to all aboard.

On one occasion a lumberjack wedged himself into a seat by an out-of-state woman, took out his well-soddened corn cob pipe, filled it with B. L. cut plug, lighted it, took one satisfying pull and then asked the lady if she objected to tobacco smoke.

"I most certainly do," snapped the lady.

"Some does," observed the lumberjack and continued smoking.

Often, after his day's run, Whorff would pole a load of

sportsmen across the Kennebec to be met by his partner, Charlie Mitchell, with a buckboard and horses for the trip to Pierce Pond.

The Mitchell group presided over what was probably the golden era of Pierce Pond Camps, which lasted from 1922 to 1941. While the trophy fish of former years were rarer, those being caught were still respectable, with 12-pound salmon and eight-pound trout being common. The Mitchells also brought several amenities to the pond that had been wanting, notably plumbing. They built two bathhouses, His and Hers, with toilets and bath tubs. These are still used by the two upper cabins.

Charles Mitchell added another guest camp and a walk-in cooler as well as the present guides' camp and kitchen. He also planted a large vegetable garden near the pond where the lawn now flourishes. The lilac bush was brought in by Guide Carl Bean who carried it in his backpack, the hand woven basket type that came down from the Indians.

Charles Mitchell also introduced the dinner bell which came from a schoolhouse at Martin Pond. These were the good, old days when guests came for four to six weeks, and ate more than was probably good for them. Their diet was aided and abetted by a cow, chickens and even pigs. To keep food fresh required a ton of ice a week, ice that had been cut from the pond in the off season and stored in sawdust, of which the area had a surplus.

The bell, incidentally, has been rung three times daily ever since, except for 1976, when it was used to celebrate the Bicentennial of the nation and in the 1960's when Jeannie Cobb fell and got foul-hooked in the leg by a treble hook. The alarm was meant to bring Gary and Floyd Cobb running, which it did.

Boston, New York and Philadelphia supplied many of the guests at Pierce Pond in those days and most of these came up on the famous Bar Harbor Express that catered to that community as well as numerous resorts along the way. It had 300 Pullman berths and made up in Grand Central Station in New York. It left Boston at 7:00 p.m. and arrived at Waterville at 7:00 a.m. Passengers for Pierce Pond then transferred to the Somerset Railroad which ran to Bingham. They were met by Will Whorff with his stagecoach and were bumped up along the river to Caratunk. The camp buckboard took over from there, though many of the guests preferred to walk the three miles into Pierce Pond rather than have their gizzards rattled any more.

Being persons of means, these out-of-staters tended to continue the British tradition of fly fishing and gradually established at Pierce Pond the thought that fishing was a sport in which the angler tried to fool his adversary and that the pleasure of fishing came from proving oneself smarter than the trout or salmon. Thus it is not surprising that the recently emphasized "catch and release" program has done so well.

The Mitchells had one son, Howard, who was two years old when he was moved to Pierce Pond in a pack basket. He now resides in the family homestead at Caratunk having served the village as postmaster and the owner of what was Albert Clark's store. His memories of camp are quite vivid and have been corroborated by Alice Bean Kennedy Giradin, related to Iral, Carl and the other guiding Beans of Caratunk.

Archie and Alice Bean Kennedy went to work for the

Mitchells in 1922, the year they took over Pierce Pond Camps. To get there they walked from The Forks down the river to Caratunk, some nine miles, where they met the three Mitchells. The party then crossed the Kennebec and struggled another three miles up the tote road to the dam, and, since the ice had not gone out, all five members were forced to trudge through the snow another two miles around the pond to Lindsay Cove and around to the point on which the camps stand. The going was so difficult that they had to leave their packs halfway around. Alice has said she cried the whole way. All of this was done so she could earn $1 per day for a seven-day week, working from 6:30 a.m. to 9:00 p.m. However, she got used to the life and even agreed to come back another year.

Alice was the daughter of Hosea Bean, who lumbered at the Thoroughfare, in the early 1900's, and whose brother Sherm lumbered at Lindsay Cove. She recalls that in 1906 she crossed Pierce Pond in order to visit her father at his lumber camp at the Thoroughfare. The spot was used for years by some guides as a place to dinner out.

Being a Bean, Alice Kennedy, now Giradin, for her first husband died in 1944, has stories to tell about guides and their ways. Her cousin Carl, Iral Bean's older brother, was a very popular guide and often would go into the dining room to tell stories to the guests. Nettie Mitchell, Howard's mother, would make sure that he put a towel under his elbows, so as not to dirty the white tablecloth. According to Alice, Carl was often asked by the guests what he did in the off season, to which he would answer: "Well, it takes a long time to go around and put shoes on the deer so their feet don't get cold."

Nettie was a tidy housekeeper and a disciplinarian. The guides took her so seriously, in fact, that Sturgis Durgin, another guide, had to resort to Dutch courage to get enough resolve to kiss Nettie to win a bet. He managed, but it wasn't easy.

Howard Mitchell has confirmed the story of how his father died in 1940. Previously it was understood that Charles Mitchell died from a heart attack while getting stove wood before breakfast one fall morning, but Alice Giradin says, and Howard Mitchell agrees, that his father came out of his cabin on that morning, saw a 10-point deer standing where the lilacs are now, went back to his cabin, got his rifle and shot the buck. It fell and so did Charles Mitchell, the victim of a heart attack.

After Charles Mitchell died, Nettie tried to run the camps for another year, but the family moved out in the fall of 1941.

The camps were officially closed during the war, but those natives who were around, including Iral Bean, said that the fishing was excellent since there was little pressure on the ponds. Eventually, in 1944, Earl, Allen and Eva Harriman, the men from New York and she from Skowhegan, bought the property and ran the business for three years. Allen served as a guide while his wife and brother handled the chores around camp.

Not much is known about their operation, except that they were well liked and did a good job. They *did* bring the piano and the first generator into camp. The latter was a Fairbanks Morse, a direct current affair which charged batteries. It is still on hand, just as is the Palmer inboard engine Armond Spalding brought to Pierce Pond more than 70 years ago, which would indicate that Yankees have been in charge.

There is one story that has come down from the Harriman regime. After World War II the Fish and Game Department began to bear down on the amount of game being consumed by sporting camps. At one time, of course, there had been no limit and then it was reduced to two deer per camp and finally, one per hunting license. One day the warden came in to visit the Harrimans and after looking into every nook and niche for evidence he was about to leave. Just then one of the camp dogs came along. Earl Harriman, ready to bid the warden goodbye, had an idea.

"By the way," he remarked, "Would you care to examine the rear end of that dog to see if any venison has passed by recently?"

Sporting Camps in General

The Maine sporting camp is at least 135 years old, for it is believed that one existed on East Carry Pond as early as 1856. The intercollegiate record for longevity goes to Tim Pond Camps, Eustis, for they were begun in 1880 and are still going strong today. In fact both ponds, East Carry and Tim, are among the few in the state that are considered natural habitat for trout. Neither has ever been stocked.

Prior to the establishment of the sporting camp in Maine, sportsmen congregated at lavish resorts and sporting clubs. The Mt. Kineo Hotel was built in 1844 and by 1890 it could accommodate 700 guests and 400 employees. What changed the situation was the coming of the railroads. The early sportsmen traveled by boat and stage coach, but when the railroads began reaching farther inland, the sporting camp became more popular.

The golden age of fishing and hunting in Maine coincided with the golden ages of lumbering and railroading. As the railroad moved north and east, they came closer to the ponds, lakes and streams as well as to the standing timber. Passenger agents were quick to realize that the trains that hauled lumber to market could easily bring back sportsmen from the city. Maine woodsmen also got into the act. They threw up camps to accommodate the sportsmen; they also were willing to show the city slickers where and how to get fish and game.

To date the era, one should know that the Bangor and Aroostock Railroad reached Greenville on Moosehead Lake in 1884; the Somerset Railroad came to Bingham in 1890; the two-footers, or narrow gauge trains, got to Carrabasset and Rangeley by 1895; and the waters north of Katahdin as well as the Allagash and Fish River areas were opened by 1900. In downeast Maine, Pullmanites were steaming to the Grand Lakes Region via the Maine Central and the Canadian Pacific Railroads. Before Henry Ford put his first automobile on the road, place names such as Sysladobsis, Oquossoc, Nesowadnehunk and Munsungan were part of the vocabulary of hunters and anglers from Boston to Philadelphia.

The railroads lured customers by publishing books and pamphlets extolling the beauty and resources of the Maine Woods. The Bangor and Aroostock was the leader. It first published a volume in 1898 and thereafter followed annually with a series entitled *Life In The Maine Woods* until World War II came along to change everyone's way of life. Another great source was *Carleton's State of Maine Sportsman's Journal*. These publications carried all of the information a sport needed, including train schedules and the arrival and departures of the stage coaches meeting those trains, lists of sporting camps (with revenue producing advertisements to help pay for the printing), lists of guides, photographs of trophy fish and game, names and numbers of successful hunters and fishermen, not to mention annual totals of game shipped by each railroad.

Travelers coming to Maine did so in a grand style. Those traveling by steamer would leave Lincoln Wharf in Boston at 6:00 p.m. and arrive at Bath the next morning, having dined elegantly and enjoyed a pleasant night before continuing on up the Kennebec into the woods. Those traveling by the Boston and Maine Railroad also left Boston early by Pullman and got to Bangor at 3:00 a.m. to spend the rest of the night at the Bangor House.

When they reached their last stop by railway, the mode of travel changed dramatically, unless it was to continue by lake steamer. For many sports, the end of the rails meant loading their trunks and paraphernalia on a buckboard for a bone-racking ride over miles of rough and corduroyed roads; many elected to walk. In some areas, sports were met by their guides and poled up river to a mid-way camp, and then on to their main camp the next day. Some arrived by pack horses, and those going to Spring Lake Camps near Dead River had the novelty of riding on a unique wooden railway, constructed from peeled spruce logs.

By the turn of the century, guides and woodsmen had swamped tote trails back into lakes and ponds all over the state. Some squatted on choice spots, not knowing or caring who the landowner was. Ownership was soon secured, which usually meant leases. Most of those early leases are still honored today.

The sporting camp plan was, in itself, a little community. The style of architecture is pure "Maine" with buildings made of peeled and chinked logs, roofs of split cedar shakes and a porch on every cabin overlooking water. The sleeping cabins were clustered near the shore around a central dining, and all-purpose, building. A bit away from the guest cabins were quarters for the guides and help. The entire group had the appearance of having grown out of the ground, which posed a problem for later proprietors who had to replace sill logs. Plumbing was "out back". Indoor facilities and electric generators did not become common until after World War II, and some camps today are still without them.

The key to success of the operation usually would lie in the hands of the proprietor's wife, as she was responsible for the table. The cuisine had to carry a reputation for excellence. Some camps had their own gardens as well as cows and chickens to provide dairy products, eggs and poultry meat.

Each camp operator usually found something to crow about. He could claim to have pure spring water of great medicinal and healing value; he could boast of unequaled hunting and fishing and his guides were always "Maine's best". Then, too, every camp had a person or two of prominence who had, for a great many reasons, selected this particular camp as his or her favorite. If they were billed by the camp operator, the going rate was a mere $1.50 per day.

The high water mark for camp operators appears to be 1904 when 165 were licensed by the Maine Fish and Game Commission. Today there are less than 50 of the original ones.

That the camp operators were no country bumpkins may be seen in the law passed by the Maine legislature in 1900 to the effect that any out-of-state sportsman intending to hunt or fish in the state had to be accompanied by a licensed guide unless he or she were staying at a registered sporting camp.

In time a number of staging areas were established in strategic spots so as to facilitate transportation to the many sporting camps that were available in the Upper Kennebec and Dead River valleys. For example, the Shaw House at Eustis, reached by stage coach, would serve as a jumping off place for camps at Tim Pond, Tea Pond, Round Mountain, Deer Pond, King and Bartlett Camps, Blakesley Camps, Camp Jack, Kibby Camps, Chain of Ponds, Spring Lake, West Carry Pond and Black Brook Camps. Carriages and buckboards would load sports and paraphernalia and head out the various trails that had been swamped out to these spots. Of the 12 camps named above, only Tim and Tea Pond Camps are operating in earnest.

Similarly from the old Washburn Hotel at Bingham, sports were outbound to camps on Rowe Pond, East Carry Pond, Pierce Pond, Bald Mountain Camps and, via the Somerset Railroad, to Heald, Moxie, Indian and Parlin Ponds. Of these nine operations, only Pierce Pond remains active as a sporting camp. Buildings remain and memories, but no commercial activity, at the eight other ponds.

In this day of all-terrain vehicles, when virtually every pond in the state can be reached, if not accessed, by conveyance, it is difficult to realize that the fishermen of 100 years ago *walked* to many of these ponds. Old newspaper accounts indicate that there was considerable activity among the many camps in the Pierce Pond area with guides and sports trudging rough trails cut through the black growth connecting the Carry Ponds with Pierce, Rowe, the Otters, Spring Lake and Black Brook. Rowe,

East Carry and Pierce Ponds were connected directly by the Old Canada Road. Even ladies in their long, heavy dresses fought their way from pond to pond and the men, despite well larded paunches, did so, too. Automobiles were a novelty in 1906 and besides, Europeans had been taking walking tours for centuries. Thus, it is not surprising to find a story in the July, 1906 issue of the *Maine Woods* giving the gory details of how one Bostonian, lost in the Pierce Pond area for five days and four nights, finally made it from West Carry Pond to Upper Pierce Pond to the Dead River to The Forks to the Otter Ponds and finally back to Pierce Pond, without food, except at The Forks on the fourth night. A very rough estimate would suggest that the gentleman, and he must have been a gentleman, for he was not too handy in the woods, walked a minimum of 40 miles while trying to get from Black Brook to Pierce Pond, a matter of approximately five miles.

Still, in his detailed account of his expedition, he did not complain of the mileage, but rather of mosquitos and the inconsiderate behavior of wildlife at night. After he finally reached Pierce Pond Camps, he spent two days successfully fishing for trout and salmon and then walked the six miles back to West Carry Pond which was his starting point. His advice to his readers: Be Prepared.

The Sterling–Harrison Camps

Only one other sporting operation has ever been based on Pierce Pond and that is Sterling, now Harrison, Camps, which actually are on Pierce Pond Stream. They were built in 1934 by Ralph and Leona Sterling, who came from a long line of hostelers. Back in 1816, Joseph Spalding, grandfather of the man who founded Pierce Pond Camps, built a hotel at Caratunk. It was run for several generations by the Sterling family and by 1900 had become a hostelry for sportsmen who would come for weeks at a time. Later it became an overnight stop for sports going to the Sterling Camps.

Ralph Sterling was asked to survey the property lines of Carrying Place Township by Governor Fernald and in payment for his work took eleven acres of land along Pierce Pond Stream which is close to the northern boundary of the township. He hired Lesca Lawyerson, who now lives at Bingham, to clear the site. Later Lawyerson, along with Bruce Gilbert, Tom Harris and Simon Cates, built the camps and lodge at an old log landing located about a half mile down stream from the dam.

Alice Bean Kennedy Giradin knew Tom Harris well and

says that he was a popular guide as well as a good builder. Folks were stunned when his body was found in the river, she says, because they could not believe that anyone of his experience would attempt to cross it on a log while wearing a raincoat, as was alleged at the time. The funeral service was performed by Parson Tom Cleaver of Skowhegan, for whom Iral Bean named his famous fly, *Parson Tom.*

Lesca Lawyerson did most of the log hewing and fitting using a full sleeper axe made by the Witham Axe Company of Caratunk. They built the guides' camp first which has since rotted to the ground. As each guest cabin was finished, the Sterlings would dispatch fishermen to the site who were eager to get to the big fish they had heard so much about.

Taking care of the new arrivals posed a great deal of difficulty for Leona Sterling, known as "Ma". She and Villa Lawyerson cooked for the sports and crew in the guides' camp until the main lodge was completed a year later. Villa's maiden name was Adams and she was related to Seth Adams whose sons had made East Carry Pond famous for its trout. Ralph and Ma ran the camps, while their daughter Mildred and her husband, Harold Smith, ran the hotel back in Caratunk. Ralph eventually got into politics and was elected a state senator. When he died in 1950, Ma ran the camps for another year before calling it quits. Bob Witbeck of Westwood, MA, who has been coming to Pierce Pond for 45 years, remembers well Ma Sterling, the Sterling Hotel and the Sterling Camps.

"In 1945," he writes, "gasoline was still tight and I took a train from Hartford to Boston, and Boston to Waterville, where Ralph Sterling met us and drove us to Caratunk in his 'Chivvy' sedan. He had a very bad heart, which he told us about right off the bat, and severe emphysema. It was a 65-mile ride and I'll never forget it with his coughing while driving like hell, and looking into the back seat talking. The Sterling Hotel was what Hollywood has always tried to achieve as a 'set', but never succeeded. The front porch was a graveyard for outboard motors, all cannibalized, sitting where the boards hadn't rotted through. The bedrooms were light, airy and old. All were equipped with a large pitcher and bowl, and the toilet was 'down the hall.'

"After suiting up and leaving city clothes at the hotel, we climbed into Ralph's car with our gear and were driven to the Kennebec, which we ferried across via a rope pull. On the west bank was a Model A dump truck that was temperamental to a fault, as it required mouth-to-mouth resuscitation of the fuel line to get it going. It jitnied us up over a ridge to a point where we were met by the tote man, again right out of the casting department. A bull of a man, still slightly drunk from his last charge, unshaven, unkempt, with a few yellow stubs of teeth. He didn't talk much either. The tote wagon was a wooden flat bed on old Model T wheels, with pretty good ground clearance, but the axle still had to climb over rocks in the tote road. Much of the route was corduroy, the rest pure bog. The horse kept losing a shoe and the hung-over driver was always lifting the animal's hoof too high. The horse would flinch and the tote man would growl, 'Maybe you'll stand still if I straighten up a few of your ribs,' at which point he let loose with a ball peen hammer on the animal's sides. It was pretty grim and a long trip.

"We arrived at Sterlings' before supper. We had a nice

cabin with a view of Pierce Pond Stream, double beds and no running water. A thunder mug was under each bed. Leona Sterling, Ralph's wife, did the cooking and as a pastry chef had no peer. There was a serving girl and a couple of guides and that was it. There was one other guest in the camp.

"The evening fishing was awesome. We had dinner at six, and at about 6:30 p.m. our guide, Hal Smith, Leona's son-in-law, led us up to the pond and landing. It was an idyllic June evening, with the sun still high over Pierce Pond Mountain to the northwest and the light golden. The water was flat, and the rises regular. The entire south shore of the pond was swamped out to sixty or eighty feet back from the water to take care of long back casts. One could alight from a canoe and fish anywhere there. This was my first crack at really good dry fly fishing and I have been spoiled ever since. A ring of a rise would appear 75 yards to the east (or west), then 50 yards, then 25, put out your fly, snug up and BANG! Time after time after time. This went on non-stop until nine or later. We caught six to 10 fish apiece each evening but released most of them. There was not the profusion of flies we have today during brief evening hatches, but they were constant for two and a half hours. We used big (#2 to #4) bi-visibles and a new fly called a Wulff.

"My greatest triumphs, to this day, came from Pickerel Pond with worms and spoons. I hang my head, but it was legal then. I took a classic 4 3/4 pound squaretail, a 4 1/4 pound mate, and a six-pound hook-jawed giant of a racer salmon that would have been an easy 10-pound fish with meat on its bones.

"I don't recall much guest activity, and it is my recollection that ice out, *not* dry fly fishing, was the big deal. Hal Smith said that Ralph would telegraph ice out to his clients, and a number of Wall Street types would hire a plane and fly up. Many of the group also brought their 'nurses' according to Hal. Pierce Pond was more robust and swinging in those days.

"During the day, fishing was typically slow. We had a beautiful rowing canoe. It was essentially a rowboat built like a canoe, but beamy with woven reed seats. The stern was broad and flat, with a two and a half or three horse engine. The motors were used only for transport. Hal rowed while we fished; a lovely dimension as you could 'hear' Pierce Pond. We trolled deep with *Dave Davis* tandem spoons and worms, and caught very few fish during the day. Guides' wages were $8 per day, from 7:30 a.m. to 9:00 p.m.

"Fishing in late June and early July was strictly evening fishing, except for the satellite ponds. Leona Sterling could be found each evening casting from a flat rock down in the Basin. She cast beautifully, and thanks to her, there was always fish on the menu. For her excellent fish chowder, she always required a trout, a salmon and a big pickerel."

Ma Sterling would be among the first to be elected to the Pierce Pond Hall of Fame, if there every were such a thing. She was a wisp of a woman, no more than 100 pounds with her Sears Roebuck pants pockets full of trout, but twice the size when her dander was up. Time and again when Iral Bean, another Pierce Pond fixture, took aboard an extra cargo of Dutch courage, Ma would take him by the seat of the pants and collar and march him out of the kitchen in the direction of the guides' camp.

Another time, when she and Villa Lawyerson were alone in camp, two hooligans appeared at the door. They insisted on entering and obviously meant trouble. Ma fetched her hand gun, pulled back the hammer, jammed it into the nearest male stomach, and cleared the kitchen quickly and permanently.

Her recreation, when she could get it, was fishing and her favorite spots, necessarily close to camp, were on the ledges near the dam, mentioned by Bob Witbeck, and at Rudder's Rock, a rocky point near Gull Rock. From the latter spot she once extracted a seven-pound trout, attested by Lesca Lawyerson, who had left her there earlier in the evening.

One of the tales told about Ma Sterling was the time she caught a mess of trout out of season on Pierce Pond Stream. She and Villa Lawyerson had discussed the matter and agreed that the taste of trout overcame the law on that particular day. So Ma took her rod and skipped down stream from rock to rock in search of supper. Unbeknownst to her two wardens coming up the trail from the Kennebec watched while she caught the trout and made her way back to camp. They then came in and exchanged greetings. Ma had dropped her fish into a bucket and placed it under the sink in the kitchen so the wardens asked if they might have a bite to eat and went to the sink to wash up. Ma gave no sign of guilt even though the trout were still flopping in the bucket. Villa couldn't stand the gaff, however, and took to her room. Eventually the wardens left, satisfied that they had worried Ma a little even though she hadn't shown it. They liked her too much to make an issue over a few trout.

After the camps were closed in 1950, Ma Sterling would come to Lindsay Cove and ask to be taken to the Basin. She was well along in years by then, but left at the landing she would heft a pack of provisions for two weeks and head down the trail to her old camps, white hair bouncing as she trudged.

The camps sat idle from 1950 to 1975 when Bud and Dori Williams bought them from Ma Sterling's grandson, Bob Smith. The Williams reopened the camps under the name of Carrying Place Camps and ran them for 11 years, when they sold them in 1986 to Tim and Fran Harrison, who now call the place Harrison's Pierce Pond Camps.

Bud and Dori Williams deserve a great deal of credit for restoring the Sterling Camps. They gave up a lumber business at Trafton, PA and put much time, effort and money into the operation. The camps had been neglected for 25 years. A lesser couple might have given up. The Williams also establishedthe custom of serving breakfast to the many hikers along the Appalachian Trail. It was a natural since the trail comes up to a hut near the dam on Pierce Pond and then follows Pierce Pond Stream down to the Kennebec. Hikers began scheduling their stops so as to have breakfast at The Carrying Place Camps.

Clarence Gilman, who once worked for Ma Sterling– briefly, he points out– and who later became an Appalachian Mountain Club member, still has a fondness for the area and declares that the trail by Pierce Pond Stream is one of the prettiest spots between Springer Mountain, Georgia and Mount Katahdin in Maine. The series of falls below the Harrison Camps is so spectacular that Gilman hopes to get permission to cut a side trail so that hikers can get the full view of the falls.

The Harrisons not only have continued the breakfast tradition, but also have developed a dinner business for down river natives from the Moscow-Bingham area who enjoy driving up for an evening meal.

Gilman's memories of Ma Sterling are not all good. He was a licensed guide, even though only 18 years of age in 1939, when he heard of a job with the Sterlings through Cecil and Geraldine Lawyerson. The understanding was that in his spare time he would supplement his income by guiding. He hitchhiked to Caratunk and was put across the river by Ralph Sterling. When he arrived, Ma Sterling pointed to the guides' cabin and told him to pick out a bunk and report back for dinner.

As Gilman tells the story, that first peek at the guides' cabin was the last view of the place in daylight that he ever saw. The hours, for all practical purposes, were from 6:00 a.m. to 10:00 p.m. and most of that time was spent washing the many pots and pans that Ma used during the course of the day. The secret of her cooking was her use of chicken fat and the process of obtaining that item consumed much time and innumerous pots and pans, all of which Gilman was expected to wash promptly. Whenever he could manage, Gilman escaped from the sink to lug firewood, empty slop jars, make beds, or lug supplies from the root cellar. He rarely saw any of the guides, let alone guiding on his own, and he regretted the missed opportunity to learn from Iral and Ural Bean, Bruce Gilbert, Bill Powell, the one-time Chief of Police for Skowhegan, and Lesca Lawyerson.

Fortunately, Gilman had a commitment to attend the graduation of a friend from Hebron Academy and so was able to get out of camp. Once on the way he decided that swimming in chicken grease was a bit beneath the dignity of a Maine guide and forester-to-be, and, after collecting his due from Ralph, kept on going. He has never lost his love of the area, however.

Otter Pond Camps and Others

Next in rank among the several sporting camps in the Pierce Pond area must come the Otter Pond Camps since it was through them that the first stocking of Pierce Pond came about. The camps are in Bowtown, which lies between Pierce Pond and the Kennebec River. In fact, the Dead River forms a bow around the northeast corner of the township as it turns south to join the Kennebec, hence, the name. The township was known to lumbermen because it had a goodly stand of timber and because the land sloped towards the Dead River in the north and the Kennebec River on the east. This made the harvesting of that timber much easier.

Because of its value as timberland, Bowtown remained one large tract of 17,800 acres for many years, excepting a few lots that had been deeded to settlers along the rivers. Names on these lots included Hannibal Brown, Hiram Pierce, Joseph Durgin, Esther Russell, and Michael Gilroy. The Osborn farm was inland, having been laid out on the Old Canada Road. In 1876, Bowtown passed into the ownership of William B. Snow of Skowhegan and Jona Gray of Gardiner. They, in turn, willed the land to their sons, William Snow and George Gray.

Old timers still remember the second Bill Snow and his

16-cylinder, chauffeur-driven Cadillac. George Gray was not so gaudy, but he still proved a successful businessman and he and Snow made numerous deals with the Clarks of Caratunk and C. S. Humphreys of Madison. These business deals carried over into sporting ventures, such as stocking the Otter ponds and Pierce Pond. Eventually the township was taken over by the Augusta Trust Company in 1923 and when that company went under in the Depression, the Central Maine Power Company emerged with deed in hand. That company's interest was sparked by the knowledge that the dam and outlet of Pierce Pond lie in Bowtown and might some day be used to develop water power.

Who actually put the first cabins on North Otter is not clear. We do know that Humphreys, Snow and the Clarks were very much interested in hunting and fishing as well as lumber-ing and that all of them were in the area overseeing their many interests. Mrs. Alice Bean Kennedy Giradin is under the impression that Oscar and Fred Clark built cabins for lumbering on North Otter Pond and that Snow and Humphreys converted them for sporting purposes. Mrs. Giradin speaks with authority. Her father was Hosea Bean, who owned a farm on the Kennebec at Holly Brook Crossing which was the first approach to the Otter Ponds. Later the crossing was moved up river a few miles to what is now known as the Bates Crossing. Hosea Bean served as tote man for the Otter Camps.

The first record of camps at North Otter Pond comes from *Maine Woods* and shows one M. L. French to be the owner and a Mrs. Robert Durgin, no doubt of the Forks, to be the culinary attraction. Her husband, "Genial Bob," and "Reliable John"

Morris served as guides and handymen. The French administration lasted from 1899 to 1905.

In 1906 Henry Sands of Jackman took over for four years to
be followed by George McKenney who also found four years
to be a great plenty. He was succeeded by Willie Bowers in 1916.
Just how long he lasted is not in the record, but in 1922 a group
of Philadelphians with names such as Gomery and Roberts,
acquired ownership of the property.

The Philadelphians were men of substance and knew how
to enjoy the good life. Jo Roberts had been a guest at the
Spalding camps and learned about the availability of the Otter
Pond camps from his guide, Will Adams, brother of Villa
Lawyerson. Adams was a man of many parts, guide, warden,
carpenter, and witness to the stocking of quinnat salmon in
Pierce Pond. His son Azel, now living at Richmond, has provided some interesting facts about his father and the high-
living sports from the City of Brotherly Love.

For starters, Jo Roberts owned the plant operated by the
Nash-Lafayette automobile company in Philadelphia and his
partner, Ed Gomery, owned the Hudson-Essex assembly building a few blocks away. Roberts was a true fisherman and
Gomery concentrated on entertainment. Both thought big.
They engaged Will Adams to tear down the old camps and
build anew. Adams asked the Cates brothers of Caratunk,
Simon and Rhule, to help him and also engaged his own son,
Azel, and Oscar Jones. This crew attacked the surrounding
woods with saw, axe and adze and provided the hand-hewn
timbers, flooring, window frames and split cedar shakes for a
kitchen-dining room, a recreation building, a half dozen guest

cottages, plus one for the caretaker.

Will and Lena Adams were the first of a series of caretakers to live in the new cabin. Dave Pooler followed the Adamses and he passed the baton to Guy and Alta Bean.

Once the camps were in operation, Ed Gomery concentrated on providing such necessities of his life as oysters by the barrel from Chesapeake Bay and a special breed of frogs from Louisiana that were recognized for their tasty legs. Azel Adams was particularly impressed by these features as he had to wrestle the oysters across the Kennebec and up the tote road to camp, only to have to shuck them. He and Russell Kennedy, Archie's brother, were deputized to catch the frogs on demand by means of long poles with hooks surmounted. Frogs in the Otter Ponds are still noted for size.

Jo Roberts also used the camps for the site of his marriage to Elnora P. Harwood on September 29, 1927. The ceremony was performed by Arthur Macdougall, Jr. of Bingham, who was so impressed by his remuneration of $50 that he noted the amount in red ink on his copy of the certificate. Young Azel Adams, who attended, was impressed by the champagne and delicious food that was served at the reception afterwards.

The Otter Pond Camps changed hands once more in 1952 at the instigation of another guide, this time Iral Bean, who had guided Sam Breed of Swampscott, Massachusetts out of Pierce Pond Camps. Sam Breed's father-in-law, William Beardsell, had been coming to Pierce Pond since 1910, so for that reason and possibly because of a falling out with the current Pierce Pond operator, Breed was interested. He recruited a few of his Bay State friends and the property was transferred. The Bay

Staters apparently had influence for the two Otter Ponds were regularly stocked by the state and the camp owners enjoyed great fishing and hunting. During this period Jessie and Earl- and Rollins served as caretakers and they were followed by Villa and Lesca Lawyerson.

The Otter Pond area lost its appeal when Gus Poulin, a lumberman, put a road through Bowtown near the ponds. He built a lumber camp on Lower Otter Pond and, as is usual in such cases, the activity created by the camp, plus the influx of woodsmen who liked to fish in their spare time, reduced the ponds from spectacular to ordinary.

One of the few people who remember the Otter Ponds in their full glory is Louise Breed Allen, who went there with her father, Sam Breed, as a young girl. She and her husband Doug are regular guests at Pierce Pond Camps and each year make a sentimental trip to Otter Pond. They are clearly upset by the rapid deterioration of the area through encroachment by man.

In their heyday the Otter Ponds were most productive, but gradually guests there would find greater activity at Pierce Pond which got much more publicity for its big fish. Dick Fagan, however, has rich memories of the big one he and Tommy Haddock literally landed one day at Otter Pond. The fish was bigger than their net, so they worked it ashore and then jumped into the reeds and dri-ki and wrestled it to higher ground. They thought they had a salmon, but when it was examined at camp it turned out to be a brown trout (10 lbs.), thus producing another of the unsolved mysteries of the area.

East Carry Pond Camps

East Carry Pond has never been stocked. Like Tim Pond and Sourdnahunk Lake (native spelling), it is a natural trout "factory," and its population has never been tainted by foreign blood. As we have seen, the pond was discovered early by Benedict Arnold and his men and thereafter was given considerable attention, first by the Adams brothers, and then by a succession of hungry fishermen.

Dr. Isaac Senter, who was Arnold's physician and who kept a diary of the expedition to Quebec, wrote of the bountiful supply of trout in the pond and also mentioned that a blockhouse had been built within shooting distance of the pond and named Arnold's Hospital, to house the many soldiers who had become ill. There is no question that Arnold and his men dined well on the resources at hand and it follows that they remembered those meals well as they were the last good ones to be had on the expedition. The blockhouse unquestionably was the first building erected in the area, but it was by no means the last.

The next evidence of building on the pond is to be found in the Somerset County Registry. An 1879 map clearly shows a group of cabins, marked Felker cabins, and Leon Baril, current caretaker of the property, distinctly recalls tearing down an old cabin called "Camp Felker" some years back. About the same time a group of sportsmen from the Skowhegan area built a cabin near the shore and called it Camp Arnold. For nearly a decade Charles Coleman of Moscow, Thomas Abbott of Anson, and George Savage of Bingham took turns running the operation. Then in 1888 Henry Washburn of Bingham and George Fairgrieves of Skowhegan bought the property and began advertising the business. Two years later the Somerset Railroad reached Bingham, making access that much easier.

The man who gave East Carry Pond Camps their biggest boost was Henry J. Lane of Lexington. His family owned the Lane Hotel located on the height of land on the road from Highland to Flagstaff. Guests driving to Pierce Pond pass by the Lane Farm, so called, but any buildings there might have been that have long since disappeared.

Henry Lane was energetic and soon had people begging to come and stay in his refurbished cabins. He became so busy that it was felt necessary to establish a post office. Lane was the Postmaster and Dave Pooler, a guide who later was to serve as gatekeeper at Pierce Pond, took an oath that made him eligible to carry the mail. The year was 1905.

By this time Rance Ham had caught his 16-pound salmon at Pierce Pond, the Fish and Game Department had advertised the availability of large fish at that location, and Henry Lane had put a cabin there for the benefit of his guests. Business was booming. Guests would spend the whole summer at East Carry Pond and Henry Lane decided that bigger was better, forgetting that his guests came because they wanted to get away from civilization. Accordingly he built a gigantic, for East Carry Pond, central building that measured 70 feet in width and three stories in height. It was made of cinder block and reminded some folks of a mental institution designed by the cousin of the bureaucrat who was responsible for its creation. Henry Lane had had it with log cabins that began rotting as soon as the sills were put on the ground. Louise Sterling Pierce, who owned a cabin at East Carry, told Gary Cobb that she understood that many of the guests did not like the new building. They wanted log cabins.

As we know, Henry Lane built two log cabins for Frank Briggs. These were called Big and Little Twin and are still standing. They were for the exclusive use of the Kennebec Valley Club. He also installed a telephone line from the camp to Briggs Landing and cut a new buckboard trail to the river, thus eliminating the trail the Indians and Arnold had used to get to Canada. During the Lane regime guests arrived at Bingham by train, stayed at the Hotel Washburn, travelled 10 miles by carriage to Briggs Landing and then took a buckboard the final 3 1/2 miles to camp.

Henry Lane ran East Carry Pond Camps until 1919 when one of his guests, Newell Mansir of Holyoke, MA, took over. He and his wife were workers and ran an efficient camp. He rebuilt some cabins, put in running water and created Camp Holyoke for his personal use. It is still standing. Mansir died in 1924 and willed the property to two friends, Ernest Steele of Holyoke and Evander Andrews of Bingham. Andrews quickly sold his share to Earl Folsom and Fred Beane of Pleasant Ridge.

Under Ernest Steele, Ella and Philip Palmer of Pleasant Ridge handled the daily chores. Ella started as a waitress and Phil was the tote man. They were single at the time, but not for long. Theirs became more than a working relationship and they were soon married. Ella remembers most vividly the news of the stock market crash in 1929 at which time Walter Hatch became the operator of the camps. His administration lasted 18 years and was succeeded by Franklin and Iris Gaskell in 1947. Their brand of fundamentalist religion did not sit too well with some guests and in due time the dining service was stopped and the camps operated on a housekeeping basis.

Title was transferred again in 1956 when Olive and Elwyn (Eagle Eye) Smith of Wilton applied their energies to putting things back in order. At that time, there were six cabins lined up on the right side of the main lodge. They were named Camp Stiles, Holyoke, Forsyth, Coburn, Sportsmen's Rest and Erskine. On the left of the main lodge stood Carry View, Gaylord, Seneca, Mickey Finn, Grey Ghost, Little Twin, Big Twin and Camp Arnold. Camps Felker, Keely and Longhorn were situated in back of the main lodge. Felker, Keely, Longhorn, Carry View and Camp Arnold have since disappeared.

Seven years later, in 1963, Henry Spencer of North Anson and Sygmont Szczawinski (Ziggy) became the owners and their administration can best be described by an anonymous guest who said: "I liked Henry, but the sink usually had an Evinrude propeller in it, and I liked to bring my own sheets."

This state of affairs lasted until 1971 when Leon and Simonne Baril gave their daughter Kathy, and her new husband, Lou Pullen, a wedding gift in the form of a fishing trip to

East Carry Pond. The youngsters were thrilled at the location and eventually bought it. This caused a disruption in the Baril family. Leon and Simonne were recruited to operate the camps, even though it meant giving up a job and a new house in Auburn. The Barils have been there ever since.

For 13 years the Barils lived year-round in the main lodge until 1981 when the individual cabins were sold to private owners. Now the Barils carry on as caretakers, living in the stone building in the summer and at Bingham in winter.

The sporting camp industry hit hard times in the late 70's with the oil crisis in the Persian Gulf and the advent of mobile campers that could be rented as well as purchased. At East Carry Pond business was also hurt by a new logging road that caused intrusion into the area.

But *salvelinus fontinalis* still goes about its business of producing fish to be caught and fishermen continue to catch them at East Carry Pond, just as Benedict Arnold and Dr. Senter did more than 200 years ago. The calibers may be smaller, but the breed is untainted.

Rowe Pond Camps

When one talks about East Carry Pond, it follows that the subject of Rowe Pond Camps comes up, for Rowe is to East Carry as East Carry is to Pierce. All three ponds once bordered the old Canada Road. East Carry Pond came to prominence because it was on the original trail to Canada. Rowe Pond Camps, some 3 1/2 miles farther south, became popular because they were close to East Carry. In fact, at one time, guests from one pond would trade places with those at the other. Residents of Holyoke, MA were in abundance in both areas.

At the beginning of the twentieth century, Hubert and Nellie Maxfield of Pleasant Ridge, the township in which Rowe Pond is situated, bought 50 acres around the pond from Levi Weston of Skowhegan and built cabins on a knoll overlooking the pond. In a short time they had 10 cabins and a dining room and, with the arrival of the Somerset Railroad to Bingham, soon had a thriving business. Guests would take the Washburn stage from Bingham to Albion Healey's place at Pleasant Ridge. Healey had the job of transporting sports the three miles to the pond via buckboard.

As with the East Carry Camps, those at Rowe Pond had a multitude of owners over the years. The Maxfields stayed for 19 years to be followed by William and Mary McGilvery of Pittsfield for two. About 1921 Edgar and Alma Nodine of Rye, NY who stayed for 20 years, bought the Camps. They never did fit into the community. Older natives who still remember the Nodines felt they never could tell what to expect next from those folks from away. At one point the Nodines tried to turn their operation into a boys' camp but soon went back to the old ways. Eventually Avon and Addie Chase of Lee bought the camps in 1943 and even though Chase's father had had camp experience, there was not much one could do during the years of World War II and business fell off.

Stanton Beane, a well-known lumberman from Pleasant Ridge, was the last private owner to buy the camps. He leaned heavily on Ella and Phil Palmer to run the operation which had been reduced to a housekeeping routine. Eventually, in 1961, Beane sold out to Central Maine Power Company which had a notion that it might use Rowe Pond as a storage area for water, just as it had thought Pierce Pond might be used.

Central Maine Power still owns the cabins at Rowe Pond and leases them to individuals. Several of the out buildings, as well as the dining unit, have been torn down.

The Lower Dead River Region

One half mile west of Lindsay Cove, the land drops away from the Pierce Pond watershed and the drainage works its way westerly towards the Dead River via Black Brook, which reaches the river just north of the Long Falls Dam. At the same time drainage from West Carry Pond flows into Flagstaff Lake. Before 1950 when the Long Falls Dam was completed, the waters of West Carry Pond emptied into the Dead River just south of Long Falls. This bit of geography is important because it explains why, in the early days of this century, fishermen tended to go from the Dead River to Pierce Pond and to East Carry Pond. Trails are usually made along streams rather than over hills and mountains. The animals had the original idea and they were followed by the Indians and finally, the white man.

Black Brook Pond Camps

About 1890 the Harlow brothers, Jim and Harry, of Dead River built the Ledge House on the road north from North New Portland to Flagstaff and Eustis. The hostelry was based at the foot of Little Bigelow Mountain and catered to lumbermen, sports and travelers in general. As the sporting scene became more promising, the Harlows put a set of camps at the outlet of Black Brook Pond in the year 1900. At first the attraction was game and hunters from as far as Ohio came east for the sport. In time, however, fishermen began to make their way to Pierce Pond via Basin and Fish Ponds. A crow would figure the distance at about 3 1/2 miles, but the fishermen, no doubt curious about the two ponds nearby, went five miles to get to Pierce Pond. This route was well travelled and was used by the Appalachian Mountain Club. The trail went from the dam at Pierce Pond to Lindsay Cove to Basin Pond to the Dead River and then south along the eastern bank of the river to Parsons Farm. After 1950, when Flagstaff Lake was formed, the Appalachian Mountain Club changed the course of the trail from the dam at Pierce Pond to a southerly trek to East Carry Pond and then west to the other Carry Ponds to Little Bigelow Mountain. The flooding of the area also forced the state to reroute the original Route 16 to Eustis via Kingfield. The Ledge House also had to be abandoned.

Not much is known of the Black Brook Pond Camps. A John Wilson from Ohio bought them from the Harlows in 1906 and eventually they disappeared. Gary Cobb and son Andy explored the area a few years back and found nothing but mounds where cabins had been with huge pine trees growing from them.

West Carry Pond Camps

In addition to the camps at Black Brook Pond, the Harlow brothers built others on the west shore of West Carry Pond, complete with a boardwalk connecting them. They also cut a buckboard trail west from the Parsons Farm, which is situated on a bend of the Dead River where its course changes from east to north. The road followed the Arnold Trail, which as late as 1936 could be pointed out in the West Carry Pond area.

The route of General Arnold's trek to Quebec has fascinated residents of the Dead River area for more than 200 years. In 1975 at the bicentennial of the event, The Arnold Expedition Historical Society was founded to reenact the march and to preserve the Arnold Trail. Some 800 persons took part in the reenactment and many of them are carrying on as members of the society. Deluth Wing of Eustis, a founding director of the society, has been a factor in the preservation of the route through the Carry Ponds camping sites and the site of the Arnold Hospital. Gifts of land by Tom Dixon and the Boise Cascade Company have given the project a big boost and the Society continues its activities and maintains a mailing address at Box 6895, Gardiner, ME 04345.

The Harlow brothers were promotionally minded and attended the Sportsmen's show at Boston and New York regularly. To stay in step with Flyrod Crosby, the famous lady guide, they had a miniature log cabin built at the site of the exhibitions rather than having one built elsewhere and then reassembled. They also saw to it that lake trout and landlocked salmon were added to the native population of brook trout in West Carry Pond.

They also were restless. By 1912 Jim Harlow was operating the Flagstaff Hotel, having sold Black Brook Camps to John Wilson and the Ledge House to Blaine Viles, a prosperous lumberman. The West Carry Pond Camps were purchased in 1912 by Rufus Taylor of Dead River who ran them for 18 years, during which time he had the privilege of entertaining French royalty in 1914 and of suffering the loss of several cabins by fire in the 1920's. The French nobleman was H. R. H. Prince Ferdinand de Bourbon Orleans, younger brother of Phillipe, pretender to the throne of France, whose cause was not advanced perceptibly during World War I. Ken Taylor, Rufus Taylor's nephew, lives with his wife Olena in North Anson, and is a guest at Pierce Pond. They were natives of the town of Dead River and lived there until it was flooded in 1950.

The West Carry Pond Camps were sold to a Wall Street lawyer by name of Marston in 1930. To put the camps back into top shape, Marston hired Glenn Viles, whose son Robert was in charge of the Kennebec River drive for 23 years and regarded as a master. From Bob, who lives at North Anson with his son Glenn, Gary Cobb learned that Marston was a conservationist and required his guests to use barbless hooks and forbade motors on the pond. He also put a barrel in a well to store live trout so that none would be wasted.

Sixteen years later, in 1936, the camps were purchased by Elwyn and Adelaide Storey, a Mutt and Jeff combination who ran a most successful operation for 34 years. Addie, as she was called, was a stern and opinionated lady who was considerably taller than her husband, who was short and stocky. They made a good team. After 1950, the West Carry Pond Camps became a base for AMC members working on the Appalachian Trail through the Carry Ponds.

To illustrate Addie's character, Gary Cobb relates an incident that took place when Pierce Pond, West Carry Pond, the state hatchery and Long Falls Dam were all connected by a party telephone line. Gary's mother was complaining about a new law promulgated by the state that all camp boats were required to show lights at night. The warden had been in and was persisting in following the law to the letter. As Maude Cobb relieved her frustrations over the phone, a voice broke in and damned the warden and the new law to a fare-thee-well. It was Addie Storey sounding off.

During the late 1960's, Thomas Dickson, the President of Rumford Falls Trust Company, purchased a large tract of land surrounding the Carry Ponds including the West Carry Pond Camps. The land was subdivided into lots and sold individually. A gate was established to keep out the general public. The Storeys were allowed to continue their operation, but the cutting off of the general public also cut off stocking by the state. The Storeys stayed on until 1971, when they died within a year of one another.

Spring Lake Camps

Perhaps the most luxurious and most publicized sporting camp in the Dead River area was Spring Lake Camps, located on a mile-and-a-half long mountain basin between Flagstaff and Blanchard Mountain. It was located about seven miles west of Pierce Pond and across the Dead River.

Until 1892 it was known as Long Pond, but in that year Andrew Douglass, a well-known trapper, and his partner, A. E. Wright, built the first camps there on a high bank overlooking the pond. Douglass had already built camps at Deer Pond. He and his partner were an ingenious pair. To provide access to Spring Lake, they built a three-mile log railway, from Flagstaff Pond to Spring Lake. The rails were made of peeled spruce logs and locomotion was produced by a horse-drawn car. Its wheels were large wooden spools that had flanges to keep them on track. The device was so novel that guests used to ride back and forth just for fun.

For a few years the Harlow brothers used the camps for their own guests until they were able to build camps at Black Brook and West Carry Pond.

By 1904 an association had been formed and John Carville was placed in charge of the operation. Carville did so well that eventually, in 1921, he became owner of the camps. Just how successful he was may be seen in the interest shown by John Pierpont Morgan, financier and Chairman of U. S. Steel. In 1925 he wanted the site as a vacation spot for his employees, so he not only bought Spring Lake Camps, but also an additional 13,000 acres plus what was known then as the Rogers Farm near Flagstaff.

Morgan put a great deal of money into the project to bring the camps up to his standards. In addition to refurbishing many of the cabins, he built a recreation building, a dining hall and a post office. Morgan employees were given two-week vacations each year and were provided with a nursery for their children. The farm, which was a showplace, provided the camps with fresh vegetables and dairy products. Saturday night dances were held with music provided by name bands from Boston and Portland. Ken Taylor, Rufus Taylor's nephew, worked as a bookkeeper at Spring Lake, and Cliff Wing, father of Duluth, was a popular guide there as well. On one occasion Morgan hired Cliff Wing to take some guests pickerel fishing on Flagstaff Pond. He provided cane poles and used a large boat that had a fireplace aboard so that the catch might be consumed immediately. Someone asked if there were any limit on pickerel and Cliff replied:

"Hell, no. There ought to be a bounty."

The Morgan operation continued until 1940, when Leonard A. Keyes, General Manager of the Morgan Bank at 23 Wall Street, New York, became the owner. He leased the property to Mrs. Helen Atwood from New Hampshire. She ran Adea-Wonda, a girls' camp featuring horseback riding and war canoes, until World War II interfered.

After the war, L. A. Keyes sold the camps and about 380 acres to the Cardigan Mountain School of Canaan, NH and another 13,000 acres to International Paper Company. He kept the Morgan farm on which there were several cabins on higher land. These became the property of Mr. Keyes' daughter and son-in-law, Mr. and Mrs. Sidney Cadwallader of Pennsylvania. The Morgan house and the famous barn were flooded by the creation of Flagstaff Lake.

Thereafter Spring Lake Camps began to limp. A part Indian caretaker, named Slim Milbery, was appointed and he used the cabins on occasion when he had guiding jobs, but he was allergic to snow shovels and in time the roofs of some of the cabins caved in. The recreation building suffered the same fate.

In 1962, Tom Tuck, a developer from Florida, bought the property. He had illusions of large proportions. He planned to build Spring Lake into a year-round resort, complete with ski slopes and air strip. Things did not work out that way. For one thing the cabins were stripped of anything moveable before he got on the scene and for another, year-round resorts in Maine have never seemed to succeed, despite numerous attempts. Eventually, Tuck sold off the property to Michael Gregory and other individuals and opened up the road to the public so that stocking is maintained.

A few years ago, a guest at Pierce Pond got talking to Gary about his early years at Spring Lake Camps. He had gone there as a child when his parents were vacationers under the Morgan umbrella. He expressed a desire to go back, despite Gary's warning that nothing would be the same. The man was determined and so Gary flew him to Spring Lake. They spent half a day wandering over the property with the guest pointing out the various buildings. He even uncovered a sophisticated sewer and water system that had been overgrown with weeds and brush. It had been 60 years since he had last seen the place, then in its glory.

The ponds that surround Pierce Pond contribute a bit to the history of the area. The Kilgores, for example, are named for a veteran of the War of 1812, who owned land bordering the ponds and who lumbered there. Fish Pond is named for a youngish hermit who spent much of his life in a shelter fashioned out of a cave in the ledges near the pond.

King Pond was named after Game Warden Ed King who also helped Charles Spalding stock that pond. King was notorious for a warden. He preferred to work in wool pants and moccasins. Tight-fitting breeches were not for him. He had literally given his left arm for the service. A steel hook was fastened to the stub.

When asked how it happened, Ed would reply with such smart remarks as "It was et off" or "chewed off" or "just mislaid." Actually it was frozen off. He was pursuing some poachers in February and broke through some ice about four miles shy of his destination. He broke his snowshoe in the fall and had to cut a limb with a crotch so as to lift the broken shoe as he walked. By the time he got home his left hand and arm were solid and had to be removed. He was 62 at the time but still finished out his career of 25 years in the warden service.

The Grieve Years, 1947-1958

Perry (Pierson) and Doris Grieve were the typical Midwestern couple who fell in love with Maine and gambled that they could make a living there. Perry was from Michigan, but had spent many summers at Camden where he attended camp and later served as a counselor. Doris was a piano teacher from Nebraska and when the two were married they took a chance and moved to Lee, home base of the Cobb family. Doris took a job teaching music; Perry went in search of a sporting camp.

A visit to the Maine Publicity Bureau paid dividends in two weeks. The Pierce Pond Camps were for sale and Perry could have them for $10,000. (Similar camps these days go from $200,000 to $600,000.) They were run down because while Earl Harriman was a good guide, his wife was not cut out for camp life and did not pull her weight in the operation. She also did not get along with Ma Sterling. Perry Grieve might have lacked some woodsmanship skills in the beginning, but he made up for it with his enthusiasm and salesmanship. He advertised the camps, wrote promotional literature, and gradually built up the business.

It was not exactly a bed of roses. The camps had been locally owned since 1903 and the natives at Caratunk did not look kindly on folks from away. For example, when the road was cut from the south to Lindsay Cove, Perry ordered a large supply of provisions to be delivered to Kennison's store at North New Portland. The supplier delivered the goods to Clark's store at Caratunk out of habit. Perry made two trips out in search of his order only to learn at last that it was at Caratunk. If he had been a native he undoubtedly would have been spared the extra trips.

Perry also had the misfortune of opening up shop in 1947, the year of the big fires in Maine, including the one that destroyed Bar Harbor as a summer resort. Hence, he had to close up and lost his hunting business that year. But Perry was no coward and he plunged right ahead, even to putting a tractor across the ice on the Kennebec that first winter. It was a Farmall Super C and is still in use after having the engine rebuilt twice.

Perry hooked up saddle bags over the engine, rigged a trailer for the machine and thus eliminated a considerable part of the strain on man and beast in bringing guests to camp. He also used the device to help Mrs. Sterling and her guests. After the road to Lindsay Cove from the south was opened, Perry built a raft and brought the tractor to Lindsay Cove. He had extra use for it, because in muddy weather guests had to leave their cars at the state hatchery on Black Brook and be tractored up from the hatchery to the Pierce Pond Road and thence down to the pond. Perry also installed a gatekeeper and instituted the fish boards that now surround the dining room.

That Perry was popular can be attested by the many stories

told about him and on him. He apparently took it all in good humor, except when it came to horses. He just did not know how to handle them. Hauling wood one day from Pierce Pond Mountain the horse bolted and wound up upside down in the hull of the old tote bateau that had been set to rot in back of Cabin 1. It took a bit of doing to get the horse back on its feet and Perry cooled down.

It was not long after that that Perry built a raft and brought the tractor into camp from its duties on the Kennebec River to Pierce Pond dam route. Perry had hooked up saddle bags over the engine, rigged a trailer for the machine and thus eliminated a considerable part of the strain on man and beast in bringing guests to camp. He also used the device to help Mrs. Sterling and her guests. After the road to Lindsay Cove from the south was opened, Perry had extra use for the tractor, for in muddy weather guests had to leave their cars at the state hatchery on Black Brook and be tractored up from the hatchery to the Pierce Pond Road and thence down to the pond. Perry also installed a gatekeeper and instituted the fish boards that now surround the dining room.

In addition, Perry Grieve improved refrigeration, brought in the first alternating current generator as well as indoor plumbing, brought in propane gas for cooking, hot water units for each cabin, and built two new cabins. It must be noted that he did not do all of these things alone, but he was the spark plug. For example, when the road to Lindsay Pond was swamped out, the telephone line had to be moved and Phil Webber of North Anson, an employee of the Somerset Telephone Company, brought in the line and maintained it almost the rest of his life.

He is another of the camps' friends who should be nominated to the Pierce Pond Hall of Fame.

During the winter of 1953 Perry stayed in camp, took the tractor across the ice to Gull Rock and felled enough Norway pine to build the #3 camp, the one at the end of the dining room. To build the camp, Perry hired two guides, Bruce Gilbert and Hugh Comber. Such was the arrangement made, and such was the slowness of the builders, that by the end of the summer, Gilbert and Comber owed Perry money.

To help him with the #5 cabin, Perry hired Dave Pooler, a Bingham guide whose house had burned down. Dave and Doris spoke-shaved the logs, and Dave and Perry put them up after tearing down the old cabin known as "Mother's" cabin. The present #5 cabin has an apple tree in front.

One of Perry's inventions was an engine that would move ice from the pond to the ice shed up on the hill. During the ice cutting operation one day, Perry forgot to drain the device until he was almost asleep, and then in the dark had the bad luck to slip into the ice hole. Knowing that he never would be able to get his wife's attention he struggled for some time before finally managing to get a hold on the engine that he had come to fix. Eventually he pulled himself up and though cold and wet he still tried to work on the engine. Having no success he dragged it back to the cabin so it would not freeze overnight.

Despite the fact that he built up the fire in the stove, undressed and made considerable noise in the cabin, his wife said not a word until he crawled into bed cold and shivering. At this point Doris awoke and muttered, "For heaven's sake, Perry, what did you do? Fall in the ice hole?"

What she may have said the time the cook left and Perry took over and tried to make some apple pies probably would not be suitable for publication. In any event, working from barrels, Perry got his measuring cup into the salt instead of the sugar.

One of the most embarrassing incidents in Perry's career at Pierce Pond came one winter's day when an unexpected visitor flew in and landed on the ice. He was George Townsend, the warden, who often came to visit the Grieves, but on this particular call he brought along his supervisor and there just wasn't any way to cover up the fact that several holes had been cut in the ice and tip-ups could be seen ready to give the alarm that fish had been hooked.

Fishing through the ice was forbidden at Pierce Pond and while George Townsend might have overlooked the evidence had he been alone, there was no way he could avoid arresting Perry with his supervisor looking over his shoulder. The judge at Skowhegan was not particularly sympathetic either.

George Townsend fished Pierce Pond himself and often brought along his fishing buddy, Curt Gowdy, the sports announcer. Townsend died in the line of duty, unfortunately. In 1956, he and Nat Fellows, a department biologist, took off from Maranacook Lake in a new plane only to have it stall and crash, killing them both.

That Perry Grieve was a character cannot be denied. He often came into the dining room in his bare feet and in the heat of summer he found a cozy spot under the dock where he could catnap away from the eyes of anyone who might be going to ask him to do something. But from the wealth of friends he made for the camps and himself, it must be said that he also was a lovable character.

Foremost among the guests who came to Pierce Pond in the Grieve era were the Bousquets — Clare and his wife Marge. They would often come for the whole season. This Pittsfield, Massachusetts couple became friends of the Cobbs as well, and are given more consideration in the chapter entitled "The Guests." Another couple that started coming under the Grieves was Chris and Thelma Hagemann from Washington, D.C. Their favorite story involved Eldred Spalding, the tote man who had come to meet them on the west bank of the Kennebec. Eldred explained that he had suffered a flat tire on the tote wagon and would have to go back across the river to get it repaired. The number of hours they waited gets larger and larger, but Eldred obviously not only took the time to get the tire repaired, but also to have lunch and a leisurely nap.

Thelma Hagemann had reason to remember the camp and Gary Cobb who, when she was stricken at camp, successfully gave mouth to mouth resuscitation and gave her another several years to live. The Hagemann's grandson, Ed Pikkart of Branford, CT, continues to come to Pierce Pond.

Bruce Frasier, another regular, virtually grew up on the pond. His father, Dr. William Frasier, was an ardent fisherman and when his wife died in the early 1950's when Bruce was only two years old, the good doctor solved part of his problem by arranging to have Bruce stay with the Grieves for the whole of each summer.

The Grieves well might have stayed on longer, but by 1958 Doris had had enough. She wanted to get back to her piano and teaching before it was too late and she convinced Perry that she should be allowed to do so. Accordingly, Perry's Pierce Pond Camps became Cobb's Pierce Pond Camps as of July 1, 1958. It was a sad day, according to Gary Cobb, when Perry walked down to the dock for the last time. The Cobbs, Floyd and Maude, had joined forces with the Grieves for the months of May and June by way of getting broken in to the routine and Gary could sense that Perry hated to leave.

Perry and Doris moved to New York state and finally back to Kingfield, where he died in 1985. His ashes were spread over the camp area by Gary Cobb. Doris has since gone back to her homeland, Nebraska, but comes back to the spot where she spent 11 busy, hectic, and memorable years.

A Grieve-ous Experience

Authors often reveal a lot about themselves. Two examples follow, the first by Doris Grieve, a practical down-to-earth individual, and the second by her husband, Perry, who was something of an entertainer and story teller.

By way of preface to Doris's story of the 1952 fire, it should be said that Great Northern Paper Company decided in 1951 to cut pulp wood around Pierce Pond. It built the road to Lindsay Cove from the south, put a lumber camp near the shore on the spot now used as a parking lot, cut a road up Pierce Pond Mountain and built a camp at the outlet of High Pond. It was at this camp that the big fire started. Here's her account as told in a letter to her mother-in-law:

"Back to Saturday, July 26. The fire started right on top of Pierce Pond Mountain near High and Helen Ponds. It seemed that several Frenchmen were in such a hurry to get out for the weekend, they left a fire in their shack. It had a good start before anyone could see it. A couple of barrels of gasoline exploded which probably accounted for the head start. There was quite a stiff wind. There had been a ban on smoking and building fires in the woods for almost two weeks before that. Great Northern now wishes it had ceased operations when the ban went into effect.

"We had two guests due at the hatchery (on Black Brook) at 4:45 so Dixon (Griffin, a guide) and I started after them about 4:15 because we knew Perry was tied up. We found Perry at the Great Northern camp and got the keys to the truck and went out to the hatchery. Our guests didn't come and didn't come so I finally called Trudie (Gilbert) to tell her why we were so long. Before I had a chance to say anything she said we had been told to evacuate because the fire was racing down toward the camp. Dixie and I jumped into the truck and got back to camp in short order. In that brief time the fire had traveled unbelievably. It was really racing down the mountain—what they call a crown fire—and we wondered as we crossed the lake whether we would beat it to camp. I broke down in the boat and Dixie kept saying: 'Get control of yourself, Doris. There isn't anything you can do about the fire and you have a lot of work ahead of you.' Bless his heart! I finally did get hold of myself and we really did a job of evacuating. Perry already had our rings and other valuables as well as camp records in the boat. We had help from the hatchery and we got all of the boats except the one we needed towed to the island. Boxes of canned food, coffee, bacon, eggs, canned milk, etc. and all of our personal effects were moved to the island (Abbe). We decided what to do about gas, washing machine, etc. At that time we had one Indian tank (fire extinguisher) here and our little garden hose. There was nothing we could do to save the camps. Our guests arrived about 6:30 and we told them to stay out. Griff (father of Dixie

Griffin) and Martha (his wife) and the kids arrived about 7:00 and Griff came right in to help. Later he went back after Martha and the kids. We stayed up until about two. You never saw such a sight as that fire that night. The flying warden flew parallel with the flames at 300 feet. It was really a spectacular blaze. We had to go out on the pond to see it. By 2:00 a.m. we could see that the fire had stopped coming down when it came to the hard woods. We all went to bed but Trudie and I didn't do any sleeping at all and the men were up and down. We were all up again before six and the smoke was pretty dense.

"By Sunday afternoon it looked as though the fire were going to burn against the wind and down the opposite side of the mountain. The Griffins went home Sunday night quite confident that we were not going to be touched. Everything was at the island, even our toothbrushes, so Monday we started bringing back a few things and we washed. We brought back the iron and I did a couple of dresses.

"Monday afternoon we got a high speed water pump with 400 feet or more of hose. Bruce (Gilbert) and Dixon started wetting down the trees and ground and brush, starting back up in the woods about 100 yards from the men's bath house.

"That night they worked around to the water tank and back towards the horse hovel. Tuesday morning they continued on around to the dump and behind the guides' camp. Tuesday night Dixon and I, Bruce and Trudie went down toward Lindsay Cove to watch the fire working down the ridge. We had six guests come in on Monday. Four were planning to go out Tuesday after dinner. About 5:00 Larry Walker at the hatchery called and said if anyone wanted to get out, they had better go fast because it looked as though the fire would cross the road before very long. The four threw their things together and dashed out with Perry. It wasn't as serious as Larry had thought, so Perry talked the other two guests into staying for a couple of more days.

The men at Great Northern were working day and night keeping everything wet down around their camp. The fire was spectacular again that night as it came down the ridge toward the cove. It didn't seem to be spreading this way at all so we all had a good night's sleep Tuesday night. We washed again Wednesday morning and just after lunch Perry asked me if I wanted to stop the machine and go with Dixie and Trudie to see how the fire looked from the lake. Except for smoke all over Pierce Pond Mountain, there didn't seem to be any bad fire except the one down toward Lindsay Cove and up in the slashings along the Great Northern winter road.

"The flying warden came in so we went down to the lumber camp to talk to him. He said it was all quiet back of camp. While we were watching the smoke billowing up, he said that he had seen the fire jump as far as our camp from the air. He had no more than said that then we saw two spot fires start—one in the cedar swamp and one much closer to camp. We jumped into the boat and started for camp. It seemed as though we would never get there, the boat moved so slowly. By the time we did arrive the fire was spreading, running up the shore in the black growth and behind the cedar swamp. Perry had been wetting down and he and Dixie had the hose where he thought the fire would be most apt to hit us.

"Let me back up a bit. Last Saturday Bruce went out to stay

overnight and when the fire started Trudie called him and he got back here fast, 55 minutes from Bingham to the hatchery. Wednesday a.m. it looked quiet around here so he went out to get his sister and brother-in-law to bring them in the next day. Just as soon as we got back to camp Wednesday, Trudie called him to come in, but the road was being threatened so he and his brother-in-law hiked in from Caratunk and rowed to the island in one of the Sterling boats. A fire warden and crew of five or six men followed us up to camp. I called the operator and asked her to call our guests at Kittery and tell them to stay home. Howard Mitchell called from Caratunk and all I had time to tell him was that I didn't have time to talk.

"Trudie and I carried as much canned goods and soap powder out to the fish box as we could get in it. We threw the stuff we had brought back from the island in the Skipper plus a few more things. The flying warden flew over and then came in and said the fire was coming fast from the southwest, but hadn't topped the ridge directly behind camp. David (adopted son) and I took a load over to the island and Perry came with the big boat towing the boats we had taken over once before. David and I came back with Perry. Trudie and Dixie took another load to the island and towed the red canoe. It didn't look as though we had a chance to save the camps. The wind was behind the fire and quite strong.

"Several more men arrived and started cutting all the pine, fir, and hemlock on the southern end of the camp. Dixie and the warden were on the hose. They got a stubborn spot fire out just about 50 yards from the #1 camp, before it had a chance to start topping. Trudie stayed with David on the dock and I patrolled the camp ground for any small fires. I had two Indian tanks spotted around and our little garden hose with which I soaked all the dry leaves around the cook house and as far as I could reach around the cabins.

"By this time our phone was out. Trudie had stripped all of the beds of blankets and new spreads and got them into the big boat and over to the island.

"In the meantime, Perry was keeping the pump going, watching for fire around the winter cellar and the guides' camp. The fire began heading for the Great Northern Camp. Four Frenchmen either got panicky or tired of fighting fire and took off in the game warden's boat and headed along shore. Trudie watched them and saw them divide, two going ashore and two heading for the island. She called Perry and he jumped into a boat and took off after them. When he got there they were looking over the things we had stored there. He ordered them off and followed them past Abbe's cabin where he had his guns and ammunition. He grabbed his 30-30 and some shells. The two Frenchmen then went back to shore, picked up their two companions and came back to the island.

"At this point David and I joined Perry on the island and so that the Frenchmen could see clearly, he handed me the gun. David and I stayed on the island and I sat on the rocks where they could see the sun glinting on the gun. Eventually they went back to the Great Northern Camp. Later that night the warden arrested them and sent them back to Canada. They never will be allowed in the states again.

"The fire seen from the island was spectacular and awful. It didn't seem possible to save the camp. There were flames leaping 40-50 feet in the air all around and way up to Caribou Narrows.

"Dixie came for us at 6:30, and when we got back Trudie was feeding the men and I helped a little and tried to put David to sleep in the big boat. The poor little tyke couldn't settle down and who could blame him.

"By 8:00 the warden said he felt there was an excellent chance of saving the camp and Perry thought I ought to put David in his own bed. So I did and he went to sleep. Bruce and Perry were staying up all night so Trudie and I went over and lay down about 11:00. It didn't seem as though we did any sleeping, but actually we did.

"We got up at 4:00 to get breakfast for 15-16 men. From that time until 8:00 p.m. Trudie and I cooked. After that we cleaned up and collapsed into bed.

"Thursday night I slept pretty well, but Trudie was too tired to go right to sleep. The fire is pretty well under control and we feel fairly confident now. We have had more men every meal it seems. We slept 37 men here last night. They were a filthy lot. They haven't had a chance to change clothes so we could expect little else. They are very polite to Trudie and me and they seem to have a great deal of respect for personal property. We had a couple of boxes of candy out in the dining room and matches but they won't take even a match without asking us. There are many good workers, but others are lazy and don't do anything unless the boss is around. They are most interested in eating. The fire warden had considerable trouble with some of them and hopes to weed them out soon.

<u>Thursday, August 7</u>

"It seems years since July 26. I pray to God we never have to go through another experience like this.

"Monday morning the Griffins brought us a woman from Dixfield to help us with the cooking. It started raining Monday afternoon and continued off and on until Tuesday noon, but it wasn't enough to put the fire out. It did help, however. When they started sending some of the Frenchmen out on Tuesday afternoon and they found out they wouldn't get paid immediately, they had a near riot at the lumber camp and they all left. We have no men left here and the Great Northern has only 80 of their men left. Tuesday morning we had 440 on the lake altogether. We are still wetting down around the camp although the fire seems to be all out. The men here, Perry, Dixon, Bruce and his two friends check it several times a day to make sure. We are taking no chances and praying for rain. We won't rest easy until it is out all over the mountain. David and Perry flew over the area the other day and Perry said it was really quite a sight.

"This pretty well brings you up-to-date. I hope you don't wear your eyes out reading it all.

> Much love,
>
> Doris, Pierson, David"

There are several veterans of that fire who are still living, including Romeo St. John, the current gatekeeper; Bob Estes, Woodlands boss for Great Northern; Duluth Wing, retired District Supervisor of Fire Wardens of Eustis and Chief Warden

Earl Williams. When Williams arrived at Lindsay Cove he saw horses coming down the mountain with manes and tails burning or burnt off. Firefighters were working from inside cabins to protect themselves from the heat. A number of horses were burnt to death and several French lumberjacks put their belongings onto a bulldozer and drove it in the pond.

Adding to the conflagration were 7,000 cords of wood that had been felled and cut for shipment to the pulp mill at Madison. There also was a near tragedy when fire broke out again after it was considered to be under control. It took 90 days to extinguish the fire officially.

Bob Estes, who now lives in Rangeley, was rewarded for his efforts over the years, including the fire, by Great Northern Paper Company. He was given a lease on a plot of land on the southern shore of the pond where he built a cabin. It is now used by his son Steve and family.

Fire is the one constant threat at any sporting camp. To date Pierce Pond Camps have been fortunate, but there have been numerous close calls, other than the one Doris Grieve wrote about.

In October of 1973, Judy Cobb Mallett was alone in camp with her three-year-old daughter Katherine when she discovered fire in the cabin only recently constructed for her mother and father, Maude and Floyd. The senior Cobbs were in Lee, Gary and Betty were enroute to North New Portland and Judy's husband, Robert, had gone to Greenville. Without a moment's hesitation, Judy called Greenville and both the Forest Service and Folsom's Air Service responded at once. A fire in a sporting camp somehow causes a greater alarm than one in the forest itself for people and property are involved. Within 20 minutes planes began to arrive. The Forest Service bombed the other cabins with water and the Folsom contingent went into action with the Scott Paper Company fire pump in an effort to help save the buildings nearest to the blaze. Meanwhile Judy shuttled fire wardens from Lindsay Cove to the camp. She also called Diane and Bill Edes, friends of Gary and Betty, in a successful effort to intercept the younger Cobbs. When the smoke had cleared Maude and Floyd had lost their new cabin and their personal belongings, but every other cabin had been saved. A faulty water heater was suspected as the cause.

During the second winter that Gary and Betty spent in camp, 1972, an even more miraculous save was made. The month was February and the time was noon. Gary, his sister Judy and Betty were having lunch when son Andy, age two, rattled the door. He had been outside playing with his cousin Katherine. Betty opened the door and Andy, with flushed cheeks and runny nose, blurted out:

"Big fire outdoors!"

Gary looked out and saw smoke and flames coming out of the gable end of the shop, where he had been working on the cedar canoes for which Pierce Pond has become well known. Here was real trouble for the cabin was filled with bone-dry cedar for making ribs and planking as well as shavings, sawdust, paint and thinner.

Gary, Betty and Judy rushed out. Gary opened the door of the shop and began throwing snow inside. Then he grabbed two partially built canoes and pulled them, burning, to safety. Meanwhile Betty and Judy had brought all the water available in the camp and then brought more from the water hole in the pond. With the two women throwing water and Gary shoveling snow somehow they managed to put the fire out. It was believed that a kerosene heater was the culprit in this instance.

Thunder storms are a prime cause of forest fires and after every one the woods in the immediate area around the cabins are checked, just in case. One spectacular blaze created by a lightning bolt occurred in 1967 when the Williams cabin on the cliff across the pond from Pierce Pond Camps was hit. Richard Cobb, a cousin, spotted the flames and responded with the other men in camp. They took the Scott Paper Company pump over but realized as soon as they arrived that there was no hope of saving the building. Instead they concentrated on keeping the surrounding trees from igniting. The fireplace and chimney remain as a reminder of another close call.

Guide Bruce Gilbert, who had a major role in helping the Grieves during the fire of 1952, was also the victim of a bolt of lightning that hit the kitchen one day, just as he was reaching up to close a skylight. He suffered a broken arm and while the kitchen received little damage, the storm ruined the batteries for the generator and killed a number of fish close to shore. Bruce's island, which lies in the extreme western portion of the Upper Pond, is named for Gilbert since it was a favorite campsite for him and his guests.

The last fire that Gary wants to talk about occurred at Lindsay Cove in the late 1960's. "Clare Bousquet," says Gary, "had a garage built at Lindsay Cove out of cedar logs. He always drove a nice, new Lincoln Continental and liked to keep it under cover. After he left in 1965, we used the building for storage, including 55-gallon drums of aviation fuel. One hot afternoon I was pumping fuel out of a drum into a five-gallon can. A spark of static electricity ignited the fumes. I dropped the pump and dived over the bank into the little brook. The building erupted into flames immediately and I waited for the drums of high octane fuel to explode. Several cars were parked near the building and were being scorched. There were tires in the building that sent up a thick, black smoke. Everyone on the pond saw the smoke and many thought the camps were on fire. The drums did not explode. They burst at the seams and burned. We managed to pull some cars away from the heat with a four-wheel drive, but some were damaged. Again the woods were preserved."

Gary still keeps his fingers crossed. A fire started in the generator building in May of 1990. It, too, was discovered in time, by Andy.

Another Grieve-ous Experience

The following story was written by Perry Grieves in dramatic fashion, which well might be expected after such an experience. The Estes family, including father Bob, his wife, Bob Jr. of college age, and a college friend of the latter by name of Don, had been hunting below the abandoned Sterling Camps on Pierce Pond Stream when a shooting accident occurred. The cast of characters included, besides the Estes family, Perry Grieves and three Pierce Pond guides: Hugh Comber, Charlie Norris and Omer Richards. Here is how Perry Grieves saw it all that late fall of 1955:

"The cookhouse door snapped open, letting in a blast of 16° air. A young man in torn pants and gasping for breath cried out: 'My mother; my mother; she's been shot. We need help!'

"He collapsed into a chair at the same time we four left ours. Where? How? When? We asked questions as we pulled on our heavy outdoor clothing. Then I gave orders.

"'I'll get the emergency kit. Hugh, better gas up the outboards. Omer, check the big motor and fill her up. Doris (Grieve) call Doc Covert and tell him to meet us at the (Lindsay)

Cove. Charlie, round up the big flashlights. Gosh, how will we ever make it through the channel in this wind?'

"I don't believe we were fifteen minutes getting started for the dam, which is two and a half miles down wind from the camp. It was lucky that all four of us had brought our hunters in a little earlier than usual for we now knew we would need all four of us this night. We had to use a canoe and a small steel boat for the big boat had been smashed when Hurricane Carol hit us last fall. We knew we would be lucky to get to the dam through the rocks to the Basin. That was bad enough in the daylight, let alone running the channel in a high sea with darkness only relieved by pinpoints of light from our flashlights.

"Bob managed to tell us that he and his dad had carried his mother up to an abandoned camp below the dam. Then he had taken off in their Rangely boat for our place only to run a hole in it at Gull Rock.

"'I pulled it out on the shore and ran for our (Estes) Camp (on south shore). I tried to get you on the phone, but it wouldn't work, so I picked up a flashlight and kept running,' Bob told us.

"He had covered four and a half miles through the woods in a little over an hour. He would never had made it had he not been in training for football.

"As to the accident, Bob's friend, Don, fired a couple of signal shots with some old, steel jacked shells when Bob's mother hadn't met them at the agreed time. He fired at a large fir tree in the opposite direction from which she was supposed to be hunting and listened for an answering shot as is customary.

"The answer was immediate—a scream!

"We took it easy through the rocks, checking as well as we could our location and the channel. A few of the channel markers showed but most of the painted rocks were just under the surface and were difficult to see. One minute we crested a wave, the next we were in the trough and as we could see rocks below us all the way through it was hard to know how much depth we had. The motor hit once, but we didn't shear a pin, luckily. Our tension eased as we entered the Basin and headed for the dam. Charlie made the boat fast and I grabbed the first aid kit and ran for the old camp along with Hugh and Omer who had beached their canoe.

"It was difficult to talk under the circumstances, but we explained to Bob Sr. that we had to get his wife to Lindsay Cove at once and fast, wind or no wind.

"'Doc Covert will be waiting,' I told him. 'Pile on the blankets; we'll carry her out on the bed spring, two men on a side. The two Bobs can light the way. It's blowing something fierce and all we can do is chance it. Take it easy and watch that corduroy bridge over the stream. Those logs will tip.'

"Every few minutes we had to put the litter down to rest both the carriers and the patient. She was in a bad state of shock and was having difficulty breathing. At one time one of the boys missed his step, a log tilted up and he went down to his hip. We had to crawl over blowdowns in one place and under at the next. What a trip! It was a carry of a quarter of a mile, all up hill and it wasn't until we transferred the litter to the boat that we discovered all of the rocks that Bob Sr. had heated to keep his wife warm. The spring would not fit into the boat, so we ripped some boards off the old dock and put them across the seats, then settled the mattress, rocks and all, on top.

"Charlie, Omer and Hugh shoved off in the canoe. We had to leave Don because both boats were overloaded as it was. Bob Jr. eased us off, then jumped into the bow. His 185 pounds plus the way the mattress was located made us bow heavy, but we couldn't remedy that. The motor took right off, but it had to be eased for we began shipping water heading into the wind the way we were. The canoe, with three men in it, was having a bit of trouble, too. They eased through the channel first with us trailing by about 100 yards. I slackened off speed, stood up and tried to make out the channel. We were broadside to the waves now and it seemed we were shipping gallons with each wave that hit, yet I dare not take my eyes off the bottom.

"Bob yelled back over the howling wind that he was standing in water.

"'Can't you ease it up into the wind a bit. She's coming over too fast.'

"'I can't until we pass that painted rock ahead. Then I'll swing around a bit. . . . There! . . . . Watch close now. . . . I think we've made it.'

"There was just a jar but the racing motor told the story. We had sheared a pin and the motor was useless.

"'Grab that oar and paddle!' I shouted. 'Keep her headed into the wind. If we don't get out of here, we'll be blown onto the rocks.'

"The oars and everything in the boat were covered with ice. We didn't dare to move around much or the pitching boat would throw us over the side.

"'Paddle and keep her headed as she is and I'll try to flash the boys,' I yelled.

"I grabbed the light and blinked it in a series of three several times, then paddled to hold our gain, then blinked a few more times. The rocks were only ten to 15 yards back of us and we couldn't gain any headway into the wind.

"'Bob, if they don't see that we're in trouble, we'll have to jump and hold the boat off the rocks....Paddle!'

"Both of us threw our whole weight into the effort. We gained about five yards.

"'Another five yards and I'll signal again while you keep her headed into the wind.'

"I blinked, paddled, blinked again and again and then—thanks to our Maker—I heard the boys' motor coming nearer. They threw their light on us.

"'Bob, grab that bow rope and hold it up. Wave them in. Man, oh man, can't that Hugh run a motor!'

"Hugh worked closer, just drifting back with the wind, motor turning over just enough. The rope was thrown and Charlie, in the center of the canoe, caught and held it while Hugh gunned the motor to take up the slack and start us out. It was a pretty tense moment, for the rocks were all around us just under water. If Hugh sheared a pin, we would all be in trouble—but we made it to deeper water.

"I could see Charlie bailing with a tomato can. I groped around under my feet and as far as I could reach under the mattress for the pump, but couldn't feel anything but water. We had about three inches in the bottom and two miles to go. Could we make it?

"'Bob, see if you can find room enough to bail,' I hollered.

'Maybe you can reach the pump from your end.' I saw him squat down and prayed he'd come up with the pump, but he didn't. 'Are you shipping much water now?'

"'No, not as much as we did, but it's still coming over the side when we hit the big ones,' Bob yelled back.

"If we can make that point near your camp, it'll be easier. Hope we get a little lull soon. Watch your end and if we get too low in the water, yell to Hugh to pull us over to the south shore. We'll have to jump and they'll have to get help over at the camp.

"I bailed some water with my old felt hat, but hadn't bailed more than a couple of gallons when it slipped out of my gloved and iced hand and the wind took it away. Luckily for me that I had my parka on.

"Our patient undoubtedly was in a bad way as we could hear her moans even with all of the covering and the wind. Bob leaned down and adjusted her head covering. In answer to my questions, he yelled:

"'She's having a hard time breathing.'

"We rounded a point that enabled us to see the landing. This put us quartering into the wind, but even at that we seemed to be shipping less water. I looked for signs of the doctor's car. I felt around under my feet again to check how much water we had been shipping and found four or five inches sloshing back and forth with the roll of the boat. I felt a bit easier for if Hugh could keep headed the same way into the wind for another quarter of a mile, the wind wouldn't get the sweep and it wouldn't be so rough.

"Just then the landing and dock were flooded with light. Doc Covert was there and heard us coming. What a man! The dock took shape gradually and now that we could see our objective, we seemed to go faster. Hugh had his motor giving its all—bless his heart—and soon he veered away from the shore and cast off the tow rope. I poled us onto the beach and it was just seconds before we carried mattress, patient, blankets, ice and rocks to the doctor's Suburban. Doc administered first aid at once. As no hospital arrangements had been made, he advised us to return to camp and phone through to Farmington for certain technicians and equipment to be ready.

"We four returned to camp covered with ice from head to foot—Charlie even had three-inch icicles hanging from his hat. The next morning we were none the worse for wear, nary a sniffle. All went well for Bob's mother, too. She has completely recovered and has the steel bullet which missed her heart by one quarter of an inch to show for her experience."

The Floyd and Maude Years

The town of Lee in rural Penobscot County is the stamping ground of the Cobbs. The family goes back to a Deacon Henry Cobb who arrived from England shortly after the Pilgrims and helped to found Barnstable on Cape Cod, Massachusetts. Son Jonathon married into one of the original Pilgrim families and eventually established roots in Maine as did many a Cape Codder. There are now more Cobbs in the area than in most corn fields.

The Cobbs also did much to boost the enrollment at Lee Academy. Floyd's father, Vinal, was an alumnus and a trustee for 60 years; Floyd and Maude are graduates of the school, in fact, met there; the Scribners, which is Maude's side of the family, are all alumni.

As they say in the travelogues, we now zoom to the figure of Floyd Cobb returning from submarine duty in World War II. Anyone who knows anything about Maine knows that cutting timber comes about as naturally to the natives as swatting black flies and mosquitos. Accordingly, Floyd got himself into the lumber business and even built a camp. As Gary, his son, puts it, in the fall the instinct to hunt is stronger than the instinct to lumber. Furthermore Floyd found it more pleasant and more profitable to guide hunters out of his camp.

Spring is an off season for lumber so Floyd extended his activities by guiding fishermen, and as might be expected of a World War II veteran he began to have ideas about owning his own plane. This idea was realized in due course and before you could say Allagash he was taking fishermen into that delightful region. Little by little he was working himself into the sporting business. But he was also married and Maude did not like the long periods from home with the plane when the weather was fine here and no way of knowing it was bad there. Furthermore, it wasn't every week that fishermen wanted to go to the Allagash. The idea of owning a sporting camp soon was being discussed. It was a difficult decision for it meant leaving an established home and three children—Gary 15, Judy 10, and Jeanne 4, as well as taking on a mortgage.

As things often happen, friends of the Grieves, Bernard and Irma Cobb of Lee (no relation) told Floyd and Maude that the Grieves, who had wintered in Lee, wanted to sell Pierce Pond camps so that Doris Grieve could get her master's degree and return to her music and teaching. Bernard and Floyd flew to Pierce Pond and it was a matter of love at first sight.

Once the decision was made to buy the camps, it was necessary to sell some 1,500 acres of timberland, the airplane, and the summer place on Silver Lake, in order to make the down payment on the camps. By ice-out in 1958, negotiations had been completed and the Cobbs had agreed to take over ownership on July 1, after having served an apprenticeship the first half of the summer. In this way, the Grieves would get the benefit of two good months of business and the Cobbs could get the feel of how a sporting camp was run.

Leaving Lee was not easy. Neighbors and friends thought they were crazy to take the gamble and Maude herself realized that this was one of those turning points in one's life. She and Floyd had moved the children's effects to the home of Vinal (Bumpa) and Etna (Nana) Cobb, Floyd's parents, where they would live during the years they were in school. On a final tour of the house after loading the car Floyd and Maude paused in the hallway. Tears were welling up and Floyd said:

"Let's get the hell out of here." And they did.

When the Cobbs reached North New Portland they called in to the camp and were advised by Doris Grieve that they were needed badly as only Lester and Sarah Arsenault were on hand to help. Once on the scene Doris asked Maude to make some biscuits and Maude, never having made a batch calling for more than two cups of flour, gritted her teeth and faced up to reality.

There was plenty of that to come for the Grieves had been gone only a day when a call came from Claude Goodrich, the gate tender, that a party of eight from New Jersey had arrived. Yes, they had made reservations with Perry and somehow no record had been made. The camp was filled with dry fly fishermen on hand for the annual Green Drake hatch. What to do?

The only solution was to move all of the guides from their cabin and send them to Abbe's Island. Iral Bean was the caretaker, so getting into it was no problem. The crew went to work to hoe out the guides' cabin to make it fit for human consumption and everyone felt better until a float plane landed and taxied to the dock. Two men with their paraphernalia dismounted and the plane departed. These were friends of the Hagemanns of Washington, DC and they quickly had to test that friendship because the only place for them was in the single room cabin with Chris and Thelma Hagemann.

But that was not the end. Another call from the gate revealed a party from Bangor seeking accommodations. The solution this time was for the help, the kids, and the proprietors to sleep on the kitchen floor.

Three days later, on July Fourth, there was more confusion. Friends, relatives and neighbors all had to see this Pierce Pond that had captured the Cobbs, so out they came and by dinner time there were more deadheads in the kitchen (24) than paying guests in the dining room (4).

Gary's memories of that first season were considerably different in that as a freshman at Lee Academy he had to wait for school to close before he could join the family and see for himself what this wonderful place was made of.

As Gary tells it, his grandfather, Bump Cobb, "took me to North New Portland. Phil Webber, the telephone man, saw us there and got a call through to camp. It seems that Perry and Claude Goodrich, the gate man, were out for supplies and would bring me to camp. Perry met me and my drums at Fleming's General Store.

"The trip to camp was exciting, what with listening to Perry and seeing all the sights. Perry was very serious that I should watch the telephone line very carefully. Any trouble on the line (two strands of open wire) would result in losing business.

"After we arrived I immediately covered every inch of the place. The thing that impressed me the most was drawings of big fish on the walls of the cabins. I ate supper that night with the guides, my father, and Perry. Iral Bean was there as were Hugh Comber, Lester Arsenault, Reggie McCollor, Omer Richards, and Elden Bean. The next day Charlie Norris, Ralph Griffin and Stub Taylor arrived.

"Over the first supper the guides talked about the good fishing they were having plus a continuous volley of sly digs and outright insults. When they had finished eating the guides got up and did the dishes. The present day procedure is more sanitary, to be sure, but it was more fun the old way. Once finished with that chore we all headed for the evening fishing.

"The second night in camp, Lester Arsenault took me out trolling for salmon and I caught two, around three pounds each. That was some thrill, considering that I was accustomed to catching eight-inch brook trout. During that first week in camp records were made. Dixon Griffin, a former employee and then a junior at Bowdoin College, came ashore with an eight-pound, five-ounce brook trout that held the state record for 25 years. Two days later Mayor Erastus P. Corning II of Albany, NY, with guide Bunny Bean, caught a seven-pound, two-ounce squaretail.

"My father was kept busy guiding and learning the country, so I helped Perry until the change of command on July 1. The very first task was cleaning out a clogged cesspool. Neither Lester nor Perry seemed anxious to tackle the job, so I jumped in and did it. This impressed Perry no end. He told others that 'Gary will work out just fine.'

"We all worked hard that summer. For one thing, the wood pile had been depleted so it became priority number one. My father would not rest easy until there was a good 25 cords cut, split and stacked. Those were the pre-hydraulic days, all axe and sledge work.

"During the evenings Lester taught me and my sisters to fly fish. On rainy nights the Pierce Pond cacophony orchestra performed. Floyd played trumpet; my sister Judy, the piano; Lester, the guitar; and I, the drums. Later we made a bass fiddle out of a wash tub. This was handled by Bruce Fraser, son of guest Dr. William Fraser, who spent a number of summers with us after his mother died.

"In my spare time I explored the outer ponds and the surrounding ridges and mountains. It was a magnificent wilderness then. The woods had been untouched for more than fifty years. There were no roads with the exception of the gate road, and only a few trails. The spruce, pine and hemlock had reached their growth and there were deer in large numbers everywhere. It was common to see as many as 20 deer in a day. "My first trip to the Upper Pond was with my uncle Roland Scribner in a heavy wooden boat gently pushed by a one and a half horse power Johnson motor. It seemed like it took most of the day to get there. We brought back two sizeable salmon taken from Bousquet Cove. My father later took Bruce Fraser, the three sons of Al Blake, also summer orphans, and myself on a camping trip to the Upper Pond. We camped on Birch Point and I recall that Dickie Blake and I hooked good salmon simultaneously, which we eventually lost.

"The one outstanding factor of that first season was that it ended as being the most productive of fish that Pierce Pond had seen since the early 1920's. Nine brook trout of more than five pounds each qualified for Maine's 'One That Didn't Get Away Club'. Three of them went more than seven pounds. The cold, rainy season may have been a reason. The following year was warm and dry and proved one of the poorest fishing seasons ever. One never knows."

The Maternal Instinct

Floyd Cobb may have thought he was taking over a sporting camp business in 1958, but he overlooked Maude's maternal instinct. In short order she turned Pierce Pond Camps into a summer camp for the children of guests, friends and relatives; a retread factory for folks who thought they had retired; a rest home for the mentally exhausted; a haven for orphans; a school for poker players; and a source of solid friendships.

For example, the Bill Gage family of Ohio came every August for many years at which time the baseball season would be inaugurated. The Gage children, plus the Cobb kids and those of assorted relatives, guests and help would play every evening on the front lawn or "tin can alley" as it became known. *Dramatis personae* would include the three sons of Al Blake, Freddie, Dickie and Tom; Joan Cobb's three youngsters; Madeleine Cobb's four; David Grieve, son of the former owners; and Bruce Fraser, son of Dr. William Fraser. As Maude remembers those days, "there were times when so many children would line up in the kitchen for a meal I wouldn't know if there would be enough left for the paying guests."

August also was the time for picnics, a chance for Maude and her mother, "Nana Kouchie," actually Flossie Perkins Scribner in real life, to get away from the kitchen. It became an annual event to gather the whole camp together and go to the Upper Pond for a noon meal. This escape to one of the islands in the Upper Pond was picked up by Gary and Betty in later years. They would go for a week at a time and be free of phones, chores, guests and all of the *impedimenta* of ordinary living.

As a footnote to the annual week away for Gary and Betty, one year they took the family cat, but when it came time to go home no cat could be found. In hopes of keeping it alive Betty and Gary asked fishermen going to the Upper Pond to leave food for the animal. No sign of it was ever seen and the search eventually was given up. A week or so later Floyd and Maude heard a cat meowing. Floyd, despite an aversion to cats, lept out of the bed and went to the kitchen for milk and food. No one yet knows how the animal got off the island and found its way back to camp.

The poker institute developed when someone suggested cards as a means of calming the small fry just before bedtime. Somehow poker came to be the dominant game which caused Maude's mother to write in her diary:

"Not much respect for the Sabbath—children and adults playing poker!"

Swimming was another means of wearing down children. There were so many that special swimming hours had to be established. The youngsters would line up on the shore, run the length of the new dock (1959) and jump in. Jeannie Cobb and Jeff Cobb, son of Lawrence and Joan, always brought up the rear as they were the youngest and still did not know how to swim. An inner tube was *de rigeur* for them. Floyd still has movies of that activity and many of the participants, now guests at Pierce Pond, with children of their own, still have the memories to cherish.

At the other end of the age scale came Maude's mother, Nana K., who was induced to come to Pierce Pond to help out with the cooking in the first year and who developed the Pierce Pond reputation for pastries. Floyd's parents, Bump and Nana Cobb, kept the home fires burning in Lee, served as a transportation system between Lee and the camp and did a thousand and one things to keep the camps on an even keel.

Nana K., in addition to her pies and cookies, was also known for her fear of the water. She was deathly afraid of boats and had to grit her teeth every time she left the camps, even though a fortune teller once told her that she would live in due time across the water. One blowy day after the Wilderness Bound camp had been established, she was found on her hands and knees crawling along the floating bridge to the new operation. She had agreed to help Betty Cobb with the cooking for the boys and was bound and determined to do it. Nana K. also became known for her flower garden and rock garden which she would tend in the afternoon when others were resting. For this she did get a reward, the admiration of a number of guests who also enjoyed gardening. Al Blake brought lilies and roses from Scituate, MA and Mrs. Storey of East Carry Pond sent the plants that went to establish the rock garden. Other guests also made similar contributions, and Nana K. was surprised and pleased that so many of the male guests had gardens at home which they were proud to describe.

Bump and Nana Cobb were equally supportive of the new venture. In addition to taking care of Gary, Judy and Jeannie when Floyd and Maude were at camp, they looked after the Floyd Cobb home at Lee, saw to it that Judy practiced her piano, which later proved the basis for her career, supplied the camp with all manner of vegetables, as well as Nana's sour pickles that spiced up soups and chowders. They often drove to Pierce Pond on weekends so that Floyd and Maude could be reunited with their children. On such occasions, Bump always found some chore around the camp that needed attention.

Hugo and Mimi Anderson of Somerville, MA can vouch for the therapeutic benefits of Pierce Pond. One October when the camps were closed they drove to the gate, taking a chance the Cobbs would be there. They had been under a great strain— just what, Maude is unable to recall—and they needed to get away. Instinctively they had driven from Massachusetts in a northerly direction towards Pierce Pond. They asked to be allowed to stay a few days so that they could restore their sanity, and have their batteries recharged. They stayed and took pot luck in the kitchen with the family. Although Maude doesn't say so, it is obvious that being with the Cobbs was a part of the cure. Others have also said:

"Thank God, there is a place like Pierce Pond."

Al Rothfuss' memory is kept fresh at Pierce Pond by the trophy fish that hangs in the dining room. He was one of the guests inherited from the Grieves and helped to make that first year, 1958, famous by catching one of those outsized (six pounds, six ounces) trout that made the record books. Upon his death his family thought it suitable to send the prize back to its origins.

Two other trophy fish in the dining area have been returned by the families of guests. There is the five-pound, ten-ounce trout caught by Anthony J. Malevich that won the 1969 fishing contest and the seven-pound, four-ounce squaretail taken in 1958 by Mayor Erastus Corning II of Albany, NY. Bunny Bean was the guide in that instance and Richard Cobb gets an assist on the Malevich trout.

The name and fame of other Pierce Pond guests likewise are memorialized on the walls of the central building. The earlier fish tend to be larger. For example, the nine-pound trout caught by Paul Kukonem in 1943 was the largest taken in the United States that year. It was a fitting tribute to the Worcester, MA lecturer, fly tier and designer. Then there is an eight-pound, four-ounce trout caught by George R. Birdsell in July of 1917; an eight-pound, nine-ounce trout taken by C. L. Young in September of 1924; and two lunker trout of eight and nine pounds, credited to Mrs. F. A. Maryott in August of 1931.

Of the 20 fish enshrined at Pierce Pond, only five are salmon. These include the modern record at the pond, a seven-pound, seven-ounce beauty caught by Clare Bousquet in 1963; a six-pound, 12-ounce landlocked turned in by Art Elliot in 1951; a five-pound, nine-ouncer taken by Charlie Burnham in 1986; an unidentified salmon displayed on a piece of birch bark; and a four-pound, 13-ounce specimen caught by Dick Bennett in 1985 under the guidance of Steve Staples.

The remaining trout, in descending caliber, include seven pounds, ten ounces by Tom Haddock in 1957 which placed third in the annual *Field and Stream* world competition; seven pounds, eight ounces, by Dr. Ferris Ray, 1985; six pounds, 12 ounces by Clare Bousquet (guided by Lester Arsenault) 1961; six pounds, four ounces, by Willie Jones, 1963; five pounds, nine ounces, caught by Floyd Cobb off the dock, 1988; five pounds, eight ounces by Clare Bousquet, 1961; five pounds, eight ounces, Dr. W. M. Fraser, 1983; five pounds, five ounces by Charlie Reiche (Gary Cobb, guide) in 1971; four pounds, eight ounces by Dr. Ferris Ray, 1985; three pounds, eight ounces by Floyd Cobb, 1988.

While the trend today is to return trophy fish to the pond—64% of the 54 fish three pounds or better in 1990 were released as against 50% in 1989 — it is still understandable that fishermen and fisherma'ams want their names to be associated with such a pleasant spot as Pierce Pond. It were as though these anglers thought of the camps as home and the dining room as a kind of den.

Pierce Pond in Retrospect

Charles Spalding, founder of Pierce Pond Camps, sits with his family in front of the original edifice erected at the present site. The darker portion in the foreground is believed to have been built by the Clark-Humphreys-Snow group that came to Pierce Pond via the Otter Ponds. The lighter portion was put up by Charles Spalding to house his family in 1904.

Above: Sports in camp circa 1900.

Below: The log railroad created by Douglas and Wright to transport guests the two-and-one-half miles from Green's Farm to Spring Lake Camps.

Above: Col. Oliver Hazard Payne, New York financier who was involved in Manufacturers Investment Company.

Left: C. S. Humphreys, a key player in stocking Pierce Pond.

Below: Guide Lee Merservey strains to hold the catch of the Briggs party which came north from East Carry Pond Camps. The sport in the center well may be C. S. Humphreys.

Above: Rance Ham, who started the stampede to Pierce Pond by catching a 16-pound salmon there while guiding out of East Carry Pond.

Below: As the landing looked in 1910.

Above: The camps with the addition of the Briggs cabin which sits nearest the present landing and is still in use. *Lower left:* Armond Spalding with 9 1/2-pound trout. *Lower right:* Charles Mitchell, Archie Kennedy and Carl Bean. The salmon on the left weighed 14 pounds, not much less than Howard Mitchell who is standing beside it.

Above: Carl Bean, some years later, in 1923, with sport and what the sport wanted.

Right: Iral Bean in May of 1938.

Above: A party arriving at the dam after crossing the Kennebec and walking up Pierce Pond Stream for three steep miles.

Left: Ma Sterling with Al Blake, Boston lawyer, and 9-pound trout at Sterling Camps.

Above: Guides Joe Durgin, Iral Bean and Bert Morris, distinguished by coat and tie.

Below: Earl Harriman with Mr. and Mrs. Allen Harriman, in charge in the mid-1940's.

Above: The camps in 1945.
Below: The dining room, same year. It was built in 1917.

Above: Sherman Saltmarsh, the pedantic Boston lawyer, with his Johnson outboard motor of the 1920's, which may be seen on the porch of the dining hall.

Right: Doris and Perry Grieves, with son David, proprietors from 1947-1958.

Left: Daughter Jeannie Cobb tows extra boats.

Below: Maude and Floyd Cobb, founders of the Cobb dynasty in 1958.

Above: Clare Bousquet and Chris Hagerman in the 1950's.

Right: Gary Cobb and Mayor Corning with seven-pound, two-ounce salmon.

Left: Typical Maine guide, Les Arsenault.

Below: Life at camp in the winter. The adults are Betty Cobb, on the left, and Judy Cobb Mallett. The children, left to right, are Jennifer Cobb, Andy Cobb and Katherine Mallett.

Howard Monroe, Maine guide, lumberjack, storyteller and gatekeeper extraordinaire.

Above: Guides that contributed to much commotion about camp.
Alfred Marble, Omar Richards and Hugh Comber.

Below: A moment of rest during the first year of the Cobb dynasty.
Left to right are Marge Bousquet, Flossie (Nana) Scribner, Etna Cobb,
Floyd Cobb, Maude Cobb, Vinal Cobb and Joan Scribner.

Above: The present platoon of guides. In front, Greg Drummond, Chris Leo and Steve Staples. Standing, Mark Goodwin, Paul Pono, Gary Cobb, Andy Cobb, Shane Nichols and Dave Peppard. Missing is Bill Howe.

Below: Romeo St. John, middle-aged (78) gatekeeper who was a foreman on the last river drive on the Kennebec.

The Guests

Maude Cobb is a people person and when she says that she and Floyd are indebted to Doris and Perry Grieves for the clientele they passed on to the Cobbs, she is not thinking of dollars and cents, but rather of the many potential friendships involved, which includes numerous members of the staff as well as guests. Maude says that she and Floyd were nervous at first as to how they would be accepted by the many Pierce Ponders who had come to think of the place as their own special bit of paradise. She need not have worried.

While it is impossible to name and list all of the friends the Cobbs made over the 24 years of their administration certain names and memories stand out. Following are several biographical sketches of guests whose claim to fame rests on a plethora of human characteristics and foibles. The order of appearance has no significance.

Marge and Clare (Clarence) Bousquet

This couple, complete with their own cabin and dock at the southern end of the complex, was inherited from the Grieves when the Cobbs took over the camps in 1958. Clare Bousquet had arranged with Perry Grieves to have Emery Hall build the cabin with the proviso that it was to become camp property when Clare and Marge no longer wanted it. Accordingly, special arrangements were made as to board and room and Floyd Cobb agreed to continue the same relationship. It was a good deal on both sides.

The Bousquets were an energetic, lively and entertaining couple, she a former nurse and he an inventor and businessman. He was a bellweather in aviation along with Charles A. Lindbergh, had gone bankrupt in the sporting goods business, pioneered skiing in the Berkshires in Massachusetts, and even ran ski trains from New York City. He also invented a gripper for attaching skiers to rope tows which brought him a goodly return. Its creation exemplified Clare's habit of keeping his brain churning at all hours. In this instance, the idea came to him at night and he immediately routed out a blacksmith and had him put his idea into metal.

Clare's energy could not be bottled up during the summers he spent at Pierce Pond and he was in the center of any building activity that took place, notably the #8 cabin, where he danced about the rafters as though construction were his vocation and entertainment combined. Marge, on the other hand, tended to get bored and would go to town when possible or go down to Lakewood for the summer theater. She did not whimper, however, for tit went for tat in the winter when she wanted to go to Daytona Beach, Florida. During those months Clare was the patient one. He thought everything in Florida was manmade and couldn't wait to get back to Maine. He considered the

Upper Pond the nearest thing to heaven that he ever expected to see.

Clare was an unofficial entertainment director, especially during slack periods of fishing. He boosted morale and kept things buzzing in the dining room. He also was venturesome. One afternoon Maude had occasion to go back into the kitchen. When she heard a noise in the dining room she peeked in. There was Clare on a ladder, clipping hair from the moose head on the dining room wall. He wanted some for fly-tying purposes. Maude said nothing until Clare had finished his dinner that evening. Then she asked:

"Was there any moose hair in your soup?"

Clare could dish it out as well as take it. One evening in the dining room a small boy asked him what to use to catch a trout. Quickly Clare responded:

"A doughnut!"

"Plain or chocolate?" the young man asked.

One summer Clare found that a certain tree was obstructing his back cast from the dock in front of his cabin. He had mentioned something about cutting it down, but Marge objected. Being of a determined nature, he sneaked out one night while Marge was still in the dining room listening to the Pierce Pond Band and cut the tree down. It could have been that the band was taking a break when the tree crashed so that Clare was discovered. However, the deed was done and he was free to fish from his dock.

The ardor with which Clare approached his fishing and his success at it are memorialized in the Upper Pond where Bousquet Cove is located. There is also a trophy hanging in the dining room, a seven-pound seven-ounce salmon which Clare caught one evening when everyone else was in the dining room.

It was a sad day for the Cobbs, and for the Bousquets, when the latter left for the last time in 1965. Clare had been failing. Everyone knew it but none would acknowledge it. As Marge expressed it later, after Clare's death:

"It is the closing of a wonderful chapter in our lives."

Later, a group of Pierce Pond friends, headed by Mayor Erastus Corning II of Albany, NY, arranged to have a suitable plaque placed on the Bousquet cabin.

Erastus Corning II

The guest who has made the deepest impression on Gary Cobb during his thirty-odd years as go-for, guide and proprietor at Pierce Pond is the late Erastus Corning II, who, despite his blue blood, served as mayor of Albany, N.Y. for more than 41 years, believed to be a record for a major U.S. city.

Corning, a scion of the family for which that New York city was named, grew up summers at Bar Harbor and knew Nelson Rockefeller for most of his 73 years, although he admitted that he and Rockefeller were not as close when they were young as when they served as Mayor of Albany and Governor of New York. In that situation, Corning gets credit for devising the unique financial plan that made possible Rockefeller's Empire State Plaza in Albany.

With degrees from Groton School and Yale and the bearing of a patrician, Corning still was able to work his way up through the ranks of the Democratic machine in Albany. He was the epitome of the old-time politician in that he had sincere concern for the rank and file for personal and practical reasons. He truly enjoyed the company of the common man, knew that there were more of them than the elite, and that they also had more children. Corning was astute enough to realize it was worth his while to drive from Pierce Pond to Albany and back in one day to keep an appointment with President John F. Kennedy.

Arthur Macdougall, Jr., the Bingham minister and author who did so much to advertise the Upper Kennebec Valley, was responsible for bringing the Mayor to Pierce Pond in the late 1940's. Corning attended one of Macdougall's Anglers' Sunday services, heard about the big trout and salmon at Pierce Pond and became a regular visitor. He was Gary Cobb's first major sport, in fact, one of the first he guided after getting his license at age 18. The assignment was to take the Mayor camping for a week on what has become known as the Mayor's Island. They hit it off at first blush. The Mayor was a naturalist and Gary was enamoured of the big woods. As they traversed the Pierce Pond area, the Mayor pointed out and named flowers, shrubs, trees, animals, birds and their songs. Gary learned quickly and gratefully.

Pierce Pond was just the thing Mayor Corning needed, a place to relax and a family of caring people to whom he could respond. He sent presents at Christmas as well as on birthdays unto the third generation of Cobbs. He definitely was accepted as a member of the tribe.

The Upper Pond was his favorite spot and he and Gary made a ritual of cooking bean-hole beans, trout and biscuits out of the reflector oven every time they went up the Thoroughfare.

The relationship was so strong that Gary never complained about the Mayor's snoring; he just buried his head under his pillow and accepted his fate. This went on for more than 20 years during which time the Mayor continually sought to help Gary in any way possible. Gary, on the other hand, steered the Mayor into a seven-pound, two-ounce landlocked salmon one day in 1965, a favor no fisherman is likely to forget.

By today's actuarial standards, the Mayor died a relatively young man in his 74th year in 1983. Gary received a special invitation to the state funeral and such was his affection for this man that he chartered a plane and flew to Albany, along with his children, Jennifer and Andy, and a few friends. The governors, mayors and other public officials in attendance were impressed that the Mayor's Maine guide would fly down for the service and even more impressed that the guide was one of the few persons in attendance actually shedding tears.

Al Purvis

The back azimuth of Mayor Corning was Albert Purvis, Dean and Professor of Education at the University of Massachusetts at Amherst and a definite loner. He was introduced to Pierce Pond by Merrill Cobb, Floyd's brother, who had Purvis as an advisor when working on his doctorate at UMass. The more often Purvis came, the longer he would stay, as much as ten weeks. In all that time he would be the first on the dock in the morning and would fish every day, seven days a week and all day. He was not a talkative person and conversation quickly died away once guide and sport were on the water.

In addition, Al Purvis came to troll and troll only. Furthermore, he was enamoured of the Gray Ghost and no other fly. To ease the strain, four guides alternated each year. First it was Richard Cobb, then Gary, then Robert Mallett and finally Alfred Marble. The chore was lightened by the knowledge that Purvis tipped $5.00 per day, but still steering an outboard eight hours a day in search of salmon or trout can become monotonous at best. The only breaks in the day came at 10:00 a.m. and at 3:00 p.m. when the sport and guide would break for one sour ball each and a cup of tea and again at noon when the guide was required to cook lunch.

When Al Purvis came to Pierce Pond, he was a widower. He and his wife had been mountain climbers and he had never fished. That changed quickly. The trout virus took hold and he became a permanent fixture, staying the whole summer. In fact, the place got such a hold on him that he transferred his residence to Presque Isle.

There was another side to him that showed through now and again; it involved his occupation. As an authority on education he had numerous opportunities, including a leave of absence during which he helped to establish schools in the newly formed country of Tanzania on the east coast of Africa. He was proud of that achievement and entertained the Cobb family with unusually fine slides of the area and his activities there.

Since Purvis always came alone and since it was not profitable to waste a whole cabin on one guest, it was deemed advisable to build a special cabin for him. It was placed on the southwest fringe of the cabins, bounded by #7 to the north and #3 to the east, and is still referred to as the Purvis Cabin.

Sherman Saltmarsh

Equally pedantic was this patent lawyer from Winchester, Massachusetts. He was a guest at Pierce Pond for approximately 50 years, from the early 1920's to the early 1970's, slept in the same bed and sat in the same place in the dining room.

Salty came to Pierce Pond with other lawyers from the Boston area, including Al Blake, Vincent Clarke and Charles Metcalf. Blake was a serious fisherman who, after he became a widower, often brought his sons to the camps for the summer. Freddie, Tommy and Dickie, and now Dickie's sons continue the Blake tradition. Clarke was noted for his patience with Saltmarsh for the latter was a slow eater, preferring a teaspoon to a soup spoon when served such. Consequently Clarke would have to read something, even the fishing laws, to keep himself occupied while waiting for Salty. Metcalf was noted for going to Sebec until the ice was out of Pierce Pond.

For breakfast Salty required 12 prunes every day, no more or no less. To test that ritual one waitress put 13 prunes on his plate one morning and found one left when she came to clear away the dish.

This individual looked like an individual. He wore the same tweed suit, knickers and coat, all through the years, and effected the traditional Boston bow tie. He also used a long cigarette holder such as Franklin D. Roosevelt made famous and would blow smoke rings in the dining room to entertain Jeannie Cobb.

It could be that Salty's outboard motor was the distraction that caused him to miss meals, be the last to go fishing in the morning and to be otherwise tardy. The motor, a Johnson, was brought to camp in 1929 or 1930 and is still there. The number of times he dismantled it is unknown, but the inconvenient times he did so are well remembered. Vincent Clarke tried to get Salty to get a move on one October day because Clarke had tickets to a football game in Boston he wanted to attend. They were still at Pierce Pond when the game began because Salty had decided to take his motor apart and pack it "just so."

When Salty would arrive at camp he would take two days to take down his motor. On the third day he went fishing, late in the morning as usual. He would select a spot, anchor and then begin his ritual of casting twelve times as though he were boxing the compass. If a fish rose behind him, or off to the side, he would ignore it.

Salty was just as particular about packing as he was about his fishing. Iral Bean, the guide, told the story of how Saltmarsh decided to take home a load of squash. People were waiting for him, but he decided they should be rearranged, so he began to unload them in order to put the green ones underneath. Al Blake and Charlie Metcalf decided they would take a ride to Pleasant Pond. They were gone an hour and when they returned Salty was still rearranging the squash.

Perry Grieves was not so patient with him. In the early years when Perry took guests to the dam in order to catch the tote wagon, if Salty was not ready, he was left behind.

Floyd and Gary Cobb were not so abrupt, but they had their limits as well. One early spring when there was still some ice along the edges, Salty failed to show for dinner, which was not unusual, but by 10:30 p.m. the Cobbs became concerned, especially because of the cold weather. They went after him near the Caribou Narrows. They soon spotted a flashlight and found Salty had gone ashore at the Thoroughfare and decided to take down his motor. By the time the Cobbs reached him he had the motor apart and the parts spread over a large sheet. It was then 11:00 p.m. and Salty explained that he would be with them as soon as he put the motor back together again.

There are some times when the customer is not right, especially at 11:00 p.m. Floyd nodded to Gary and they pinned Salty to the ground. While Gary held the victim, Floyd folded up the sheet with the motor parts and put it into the boat. Then the two of them wrestled Salty into it and headed for camp. He wasn't happy, but neither were Floyd and Gary.

Charlie Metcalf

Charlie was another Massachusetts barrister who came to camp with Saltmarsh *et al*. He and his wife Rita would spend the summer in the Bousquet camp. They were members of the codfish aristocracy. They lived in a 1670 house filled with antiques in Rowley, MA and not far from the cemetery in which generations of Metcalfs were buried. Charlie was Clerk of the Court at Salem and loved to show visitors the original documents of the Salem Witch Trials, written on parchment with a quill pen. Charlie and Rita also were responsible for enticing the Burkes, Joe and Joan, of Rowley, into tasting the pleasures of Pierce Pond Camps.

Charlie Reiche

This journalist, publicist and man of the world made a special impact on Pierce Pond and the Cobb family, just as they apparently did on him. To quote Maude Cobb:

"We owe a debt of gratitude to the person who referred Charlie Reiche to Pierce Pond. He and his wife were fishing on the Kennebec in the Bingham area, when he heard about Pierce Pond and the camps. That began an association that lasted for 22 years.

"Charlie was blustery, abrupt, opinionated, critical, and sometimes uncomplimentary, but he proved to be an ardent booster of Pierce Pond and a very special friend of all of the Cobbs. It would be hard to compute the financial benefits that evolved from Charlie's advertising. Many individuals, several families, fishermen, hunters, summer vacationers, children who worked, children who attended Wilderness Bound found their way to Cobb's Camps through him, directly or indirectly.

"Soon Charlie was coming several times a year. Upon retirement he moved from Connecticut, where he had been active in conservation, to Brunswick, which was much nearer Pierce Pond and in which Jean and Leon Spinney, old Pierce Pond friends, lived. He had been an editor for the *Washington Post* and for the *Providence Journal*. Later his residence in Connecticut gave him the opportunity to contribute to the cause of conservation in that state. He was instrumental in the watershed project there and also took advantage of the fishing available nearby.

"In addition to his newspaper work, Charlie also did publicity for sporting companies and wrote articles for sporting magazines. Accordingly he missed few chances to make fishing trips to exotic climes and territories. It was not surprising that he was the one to introduce nymph fishing to Pierce Pond. He had studied fly fishing most of his life and from his magazine contacts was aware of the latest developments in the field.

"For all of his worldliness, Charlie was at home in the camp kitchen. He loved to eat with Floyd and Gary and he was a favorite of Jeannie's. He would spend hours talking while we went about our work.

"Always after a visit, we could expect a gracious letter thanking us for making his trip so enjoyable. One letter we have always remembered contained a hilarious account of his getting mixed up in a doll parade in Madison on Memorial Day.

"Charlie quickly learned that I liked to read and do crossword puzzles, so I usually could expect a gift, more often a book, and most always a Maine book. He discovered Esther Wood, the *Ellsworth American* columnist, and knowing that Gary, Betty and Judy had been graduated from Gorham where she taught, he bought her books as well as E. B. White's. Once he told me that a certain bookstore had x number of books on Maine. I think he took the trouble to count them, knowing it was one of my interests. Once, to my delight, he came up with a big Webster's dictionary. He figured that it would have any word likely to turn up in a crossword puzzle.

"Charlie thought that Howard Monroe, the gatekeeper, was an especially attractive character and even quoted him in some of his magazine articles, complete with expletives, like:

"'They ought to hang the B———s, burn the books, and start over again.'

"'They didn't know enough to pound sand into a knothole.'

"He made several trips to Lee and to North New Portland

during the winter as a way of biding his time until ice out so he could go back to fishing. His most favorite place was Pickerel Pond, and that is where he wanted his ashes to be spread.

"Somehow his old typewriter, the one he used in his professional life and to type his many letters to Pierce Pond, got to Pierce Pond and when he was gone, it seemed a shame to discard it, so we took it back home to Lee. He also left us the bulk of his fishing library."

Helen Schlaak, a Pierce Pond habituee who also lives in Brunswick, recalls that when Charlie Reiche died in 1987, at age 75, a group of his friends banded together and published a book of his letters as a sort of memorial.

The Monico Family

Four generations of this family have fished at Pierce Pond and all four are represented on the 34 boards in the dining area which depict those stout fishermen and fisherma'ams who boated trout or salmon weighing three pounds or more. Frank M. Monico, Sr. was the patriarch of the group and he predates the advent of Cobbs at Pierce Pond. He knew Floyd when the latter was guiding out of Lee and he followed the senior Cobb when he took over the Pierce Camps in 1958.

Frank was a mason and plasterer from Connecticut and he trained his children in the way they should go, for son Moe came to the pond early in his life and became Floyd Cobb's best friend. Frank also constructed the fireplace in the dining room and fittingly ended his life while on a fishing trip to Pierce Pond. He had a fatal heart attack while fishing with his grandson Frankie. The latter followed through and brought his son

Evan to the camps, also at an early age. Evan proved his worth in 1990, when he made the "boards" at age 7.

The esteem in which the Cobbs and Pierce Pond Camps are held can be attested by the difficulty encountered by newcomers in getting reservations and the continued patronage of the old timers. The intercollegiate record for regular attendance currently is held by Morgan Daboll of Salem, CT who has been coming north for 54 years, except for World War II when the camps were closed. That means that he was entertained by the Mitchells, the Harrimans, the Grieves and two generations of Cobbs.

He is followed by Dick Fagan of Kenniston, CT, at 53 years; Bob Witbeck of Westwood, MA, 47 years, including some time at the Sterling camps; and Emile Gaulien of Warwick, RI, 47 years.

Other guests with high marks for loyalty include Tony Jonklas of Thomasville, GA and the Fuller brothers, Bob from Dover, MA and Ben from Alexandria, VA. Maude Cobb's brother Claude used to guide the Fuller brothers and they have occasion in these later years to stop by in Lee to see him. It's hard to get the Cobbs out of one's system.

Guests entitled to wear 30-year hash marks include Alan Case of New Milford, CT; Roger Dabold, Jr., Salem, CT; Ed Kluck, Hamden, CT; Walt McDonough, Chelsea, MA; Robert Morrell, Brunswick, ME; Charles and Marion Reeves, Winchester, MA; Carl Schofield, Lynn, MA; and Hobart Warner, Danbury, CT. In addition there are six hunters from Ridgewood, NJ who have come to Pierce Pond for at least three decades. They include Joe Dockray, John Fiorillo, John Pruiksma,

George Reinhart, Joe Sheffel, Jr., and Al Vandenberg.

Not all guests fall into the "most wanted" category. There was the gentleman who decided that Pierce Pond was an ideal place for a binge and proceeded to drink himself into obnoxiousness. Floyd Cobb escorted him to the gate. The parting was pleasant enough. In fact, the chastened guest even paid Floyd a compliment.

"Mr. Cobb," he said, "I want you to know that I have never been thrown out of a nicer place."

Then there was the guest who drove Iral Bean to distraction. Iral's solution was to leave the gentleman on Mayor's Island without a boat. On his return to camp, Iral informed Floyd Cobb that there was a limit to his patience and as far as he was concerned said guest could stay on the island until the pond froze over.

Other guests who have been coming regularly to Pierce Pond for 30 or more years include The American Meter Company party from Boston; Richard Childs, Holden, MA; the Bill Gage Family, Mansfield, OH; Willie Jones, Putnam, CT; Pete and Lee Karotie, Bristol, CT; Ed Kluck, Hamden, CT; Paul and Lillian Lepore, Marlboro, MA; Carl Merrill, Cape Neddick, ME; Ethel Peck, Detroit, ME; Carroll Ross, Falmouth, ME; Victor Staknis, Watertown, MA; John and David Wallace, Lexington, MA; and Bob and Blanche Wilson, Portland, ME.

Maude Cobb must have been a good boss because, in addition to many guests, lots of former staff members still keep in touch. The names tumble from Maude's lips: Cora Longley, who worked for the Grieves and now lives in Embden; her husband Dick, a former warden; the Hermes family, Joel, who was Gary's first applicant for Wilderness Bound and his sister Mary, who dreamed of working at Pierce Pond, and finally did; Ruth Coffin of Lee who, when she learned that Maude was ill, greeted Floyd in the kitchen with: "Well, sonny, I guess it's up to you and me today."

Then there were the many Cobbs, some related, some not: Lawrence and Joan (related), who came to help out for a while and stayed eight or so years; their children, Jeff, Delia and Larry; Joan's niece, Judy Thompson; Joan's sister, Madeline, and her children Derrick and Debby; Marguerite Cobb, mother of Richard, first cousin of Floyd; and David Harmon, who married Mary Hermes; Lester and Sarah Arsenault, valuable carryovers from the Grieves; and even Doris herself, who makes it back on occasion.

Pierce Pond may some day be renamed Mecca.

The Gary and Betty Years

Anyone who has been privileged to view the present day operation of Pierce Pond Camps at close hand has got to be impressed with the manner in which things seem to get done. There may be crises, but the average guest is not aware of them. You ask Gary a question and the answer usually is:

"Yup."

You'd think he'd say "no" once in a while and maybe he does, but he gives the appearance of having everything under control. He doesn't even let his pipe upset him the way some smokers do. Usually a pipe smoker has to do something with a pipe—clean it, knock out ashes, light it, point with it, fill it, or just fidget with it. Not Gary. He simply smokes his as though he had no cares at all.

This laid back attitude has a solid basis. For one thing, Gary has spent most of his adult life at Pierce Pond. He has seen about everything happen that is likely to happen in a sporting camp and he is well equipped to handle any situation. Furthermore, he and Betty have worked so long together that they know who is supposed to do what and when. They work like a veteran doubles team in tennis, instinctively moving into the right place at the right time. Yet while Gary is standing around talking with guests as though he had nothing else on his mind, Betty is in the kitchen constantly moving, answering questions from the staff and suggesting that Suzy might care to peel some potatoes or whip up a mess of hot biscuit.

After 33 years of camp life, starting at age 15 in 1958 when his father took over Pierce Pond Camps, Gary can be described as well seasoned. He has been guiding since he was 18 and with one exception, has spent part or all of every summer at the place, as well as two winters.

For the record, Gary was graduated from Lee Academy in 1960 and immediately enrolled at what was then Gorham State Teachers College, where he met Betty Verrill of Gray, an event that Gary describes as the best thing that ever happened to him and to Pierce Pond. During college Betty was introduced to Pierce Pond which may have convinced her that Gary was the right guy. There may have been a question in 1962 when Gary took a job on the West Coast, cutting Douglas Fir in Washington, at the suggestion of a Scott Paper Company executive, who had the mistaken idea that he could convince Gary that he was made for the lumber business.

Gary and Betty were graduated from Gorham in 1964 and promptly got engaged. Maude Cobb well remembers the summer night that Gary, armed with a ring specially made for him by Paul Sydney, a jeweler who was a guest at the camps, took Betty for a canoe ride. It was the kind of situation that romantic novelists like to describe, but seemed the natural thing to do under the circumstances. Where else in a fishing camp is one able to find peace and quiet, but out in the middle of the pond?

Once married, Gary and Betty signed on with the Millinocket school system where they taught for five years in the lower grades. Each summer, however, they returned to Pierce Pond and the camping virus got to them. They made the move in 1969 and have been there ever since, happy as clams at high tide, or perhaps it would be better to say happy as loons when the smelt are running.

Although fishing is the more popular sport under the Cobbs, Gary, like his father, has a penchant for hunting. He enjoys exploring new territory, although there no longer is much of that in the area, and he revels in the freedom one feels when treking and tracking. It was this love of the outdoors that led him to open up the Wilderness Bound Camp across the cove in the same year he and Betty returned. They started with six boys, some old canoes and a dump truck, but the idea caught on and was most successful for 17 years.

As a teacher, Gary wanted to give his young charges the rigorous discipline of Outward Bound with an opportunity to learn about the Maine woods and its mammal and aquarian population. He eventually divided his groups into Junior Voyageurs (11-12 years), Voyageurs (13-14 years) and Senior Voyageurs (14-16 years). The youngest group stayed close to Pierce Pond with side trips along the Appalachian Trail, to the Upper West Branch of the Penobscot River and to the Moose River. The Voyageurs and the Senior Voyageurs, after five days of training at the base camp, would then move out to such locations as the Dead River, the Allagash, the St. John and the

East Branch of the Penobscot as well as the Katahdin and Bigelow Ranges. From these bases the two groups would be separated for medium and more difficult adventures.

In short, Gary was passing along to his young guests—from 30-36 each summer—the experience he had accumulated in the woods. They were given a taste of the life of a woodsman, from baking bean hole beans to tying flies and catching trout and salmon. Backpacking and portaging were included although more as something to be experienced rather than enjoyed.

While Gary was handling the activities of the program, with an assist from Jim Miller who served as head guide for the older boys and Peter Brawn, another Millinocket teacher, Betty was getting her experience as a restaurateur. She did the ordering and cooking for Wilderness Bound and had help from Maude's mother, Flossie Scribner (the one who was skittish about walking over the bridge to the island camp), from Gary's cousin, Diane Scribner, and from Cheryl Arsenault, Cathy Taylor and Jennifer Cobb.

Just how successful the program was can be seen in the number of former campers and guides who stay in touch with the Cobbs. Rich Edgerly and Brad Worth, former dock boys, get back whenever they can. Chris Leo and Steve Staples, who served as trip leaders for Wilderness Bound, are now regular guides at Pierce Pond. Greg Drummond and Paul Pono, who served as guides for Wilderness Bound are doing the same thing for Gary now that he is in charge of the camp operation. Charles Gill and Igor Sikorski, former campers, make sure to get back whenever possible.

As if this were not enough, Gary and Betty decided to

spend the winters of 1971 and 1972 in camp, along with Jennifer 3, Andy 1, Gary's sister Judy, her husband Robert Mallett and their daughter Katherine, age 1. That certainly had to be a test of devotion, but it was passed successfully. Gary admits that it was rugged, especially travelling in and out of camp in sub-zero weather with three small children. What may have halted the activity was the long spring of 1972, since ice-out did not come until May 20. To bring in some cash, Gary and Robert trapped, mostly beaver. They made about $1,500 all told.

The beaver business created at least one highlight. It seems that once the pelts had been removed the carcuses were left out of doors in natural refrigeration until such time as bait was needed for the traps. Since there was a plethora of beaver and since daughter Jennifer had a minimum of companions her own age, it is not surprising that the *corpora dilecti* became playthings. Jennifer's active imagination saw them as guests at a tea party and several of them were thus seated around an imaginary tea table. Whom else could she ask? Andy was too small and preferred to hold birdseed in his hand for the chickadees, and the older folks were too busy.

Gary and Robert also started building Grand Laker canoes of cedar, those sleek, handsome craft the guides and special guests own and use, and which are a trademark of Pierce Pond. The business was later turned over to Greg Drummond, the popular guide, whose wife Pat and family form the bulwark of Betty's kitchen crew. Like the Cobb children, the Drummond girls were taught early that helping around the kitchen and dining room is fun.

As Gary began to take over more and more responsibility

for operating Pierce Pond Camps, the pressure of running two operations became too much so that 1986 was the last year that Wilderness Bound was open. However, all of the equipment has been stored away and it is entirely possible that son Andy, now in college, well might start it up again one day.

The actual transition from the Floyd-Maude team to that of Gary-Betty came in 1982 and was made in a smooth and efficient manner. Gary and Betty were more than adequately prepared for the job. They also inherited a most capable crew, including Greg and Pat Drummond, guide and utility infielder, respectively, of Highland; Janette Doane of Kingman, who helped with the cooking; Carole Pinkham, from Lexington, who was a cabin girl under Floyd and Maude and now helps in the kitchen; and Mary Ellen Durrell of Kingfield, who trained as a teacher, wound up as a buyer for Sugarloaf in the winter and spends her summer vacations dealing meals off her hip and trading smart remarks with the guests at Pierce Pond.

As might be expected in a family business, children Jennifer and Andy are part of the staff as is Judy Cobb Mallett's daughter Katherine. Other helpers include Becky Davis, a friend of Jennifer, and Shane Nichols, a friend of Andy and son of Pam and Pete Nichols of Kingfield. The latter is a woodsman who takes off during the mud season to help the Cobbs open up camp. His wife Pam also comes to the aid of the camp operators as does Pam's brother Bill Howe, who comes in to guide on occasion.

This litany of friends and relatives helps to explain the smoothness of the Cobb operation. As Gary and Betty put it:

"We wouldn't think of hiring anyone we did not know."

There is another factor in the success of the Cobb organization that must not be overlooked. Because of the family feeling among those involved in the daily operations, there has developed a team spirit that makes sure that certain unwritten rules are applied. Examples include the one that after each rain, every boat must be bailed; that all laundry must be taken down and folded by 4 p.m. each day; that every fisherman must be met at the dock, whether arriving from civilization, or returning from fishing, whatever the hour.

One Year at a Time

The year at Pierce Pond begins the end of January when Gary and Betty gather their friends for an "icing bee." By then the ice on the pond has reached a good 16 to 18 inches and will take snowmobiles, pickup trucks and most anything else that needs to be taken to camp the easy way. Depending on the winter, Gary might have to plow all the way from the state road through the gate and down to Lindsay Cove. He keeps on going, all things being equal, and makes a road across the pond and right up to the ice house.

That phrase, "depending on the winter," covers a lot of territory. One winter the road from North New Portland was closed for a week and the crews had to borrow a huge snow blower from Aroostook County in order to get things cleared up. There were 20 feet of snow on the ground and the Cobbs took a picture of a snowmobile on the roof of cabin #5 (the one by the apple tree).

The icing bee is a one day affair. Some two dozen, baker's or otherwise, friends and relatives join in to cut about 200 cakes, 18 x 18 inches square, with chain saws as starters and then the old fashioned saws which take to water better than the modern utensil. Participants include Andy Cobb, Shane Nichols, Andy's boyhood friend and now a licensed guide working at the pond, Greg and Pat Drummond and Gerry and Jean Morton, proprietors of Morton's General Store at North New Portland. Ricky Wallace comes from Connecticut for the occasion and Chassy Gill, a former Wilderness Bound camper, from Portland. Rick is so impressed with the amount of work involved he never takes any ice from the camp on his fishing trips. Instead he waits until he gets to Morton's store before he ices his fish.

Having lived for two winters at Pierce Pond, Gary and Betty know how to operate there in cold weather. They furnish their cabin with cooking facilities and they get their water from the ice hole made by the cutters. Once the ice is cut it is carted up to the ice house by means of a four-wheel drive pickup truck. Sawdust comes from a local mill at Highland, just north of North New Portland. In the old days before mechanical refrigeration, it took four or five days to get enough ice stored away. Then it was considered work, not a bee or an outing as it is now.

Gary keeps coming into the camps all winter, about two or three times a week, largely because he just loves the place and is happiest when there. On occasion he shovels off the roofs, again, depending on the winter. At this time of year he also brings in any heavy supplies, such as lumber, stove piping, roofing, etc. over the ice.

The real action begins in mid-April before the ice goes out. It is something of a trick to get in as the ice is no longer strong enough to hold vehicles, so Gary, Betty *et al* have to walk about a mile and a quarter from Lindsay Cove. Camp openers include Greg and Pat Drummond and their girls; Pete Nichols, father of Shane; and Carole Pinkham. The purpose of the trip is to clean the cabins of their winter accumulation. Ceilings and walls are swept and the walls washed and curtains and bedspreads are gathered for washing. Then the crew goes home for a few days, except for Carole, now virtually a member of the family, who stays on alone to answer the phone and continue the spring cleaning.

The only incident that bothered Carole in recent years was a leak in cabin #1. She found water on the floor, discovered where the trouble was and scratched her head as to what to do next. The break was at the incoming elbow of the pipe and she looked around for some way other than her finger, which she tried for a while, with which to plug the pipe. Finally, in desperation she spotted a corn cob pipe that Gerry Morton had left behind and jammed that into the opening. Betty Cobb appeared after a time. She didn't know where the shut-off valve was, but she did know where to find some duct tape, so a jury rig of tape and corn cob pipe served until help could be had.

Only two people know where the 50-odd cut-off valves are in the camps, for the place just growed like Topsy and no one has ever drawn a plan of the water system. Floyd and Gary have been around long enough to know from experience and neither was at camp. The temperature was below 32 degrees and the gals were concerned. The crisis passed when Floyd, heading into camp, called from North New Portland. He was able to describe where the water could be turned off.

As Gary says, the only way a map of the system might be

made would be in the event the camps were to be sold and Betty emphasizes that that is not even a remote possibility.

Near ice-out, and Jahveh himself never knows when that will be, the crew irons curtains and bedspreads and makes up beds. Meanwhile the eager beavers begin calling in.

"When is ice-out?"

First in line, usually, are Charles Burnham, Joe Burke, Willie Jones and Vic Staknis. Some don't wait for the word, but come right in anyway. Once in a while an eager guest will get to camp before the food supplies. As D-Day approaches, trips are made out to North New Portland or Madison for food supplies. This year (1991) camp opened for guests on Thursday, May 2, which meant that lobsters had to be ordered the day before and picked up at Madison. Meats come from Jordan's at Bangor and case goods and produce are got from Morton's and Shop and Save.

Betty orders her supplies a week at a time for an average of 35 guests and an expandable, but not expendable, crew. For seven days, she plans to use 40 dozen eggs, 30 pounds of oleo, 100 pounds of flour, 30 pounds of sugar, a gallon of molasses (Crosby's), a gallon of pickles, 27 packages of yeast, 100 pounds of potatoes (hand-picked for her by a friendly farmer in Lee), and 25 pounds of onions. On a daily basis the kitchen crew will turn out 12-15 loaves of bread and 80 cookies. It takes a heap of cooking to make the place a home.

Making reservations at Pierce Pond for early spring is a gamble. If the ice fails to go out, it's just too bad. Gary will try to squeeze you in later, but there isn't much room. And ice-out over the last 38 years has ranged from April 21 (1987) to May 20

(1972). For the most part it comes between May 6-8, but since 1974 the trend has been towards earlier dates. If the guests arrive before the ice goes out, they just stay, no matter how long it takes. Being at Pierce Pond is what they want, fishing or no fishing.

Any time that Gary can get before the season starts is so much gravy for the winter can do much damage to docks (five of them), the seven miles of road and telephone wire, as well as 20 boats and motors and three generators. The telephone wire is the most vulnerable. It can get torn by animals, lumber trucks and even vandals. There is brush to be cut, trails to the ponds cleared and culverts to be replaced, not to mention repairing washouts on the road.

To quote Gary:

"There is much to look after and keep in order and it seems that when everything is looking and running well, then comes the time to put it all to sleep again."

Once the season gets started, one week is pretty much like another. About the only things that break the even tenor of the summer are winds and thunder storms. Most folks show up on schedule and those who don't, call well in advance to warn the Cobbs. Health is the main factor in such aberrations.

The fishing season ends on September 30 and then comes the process of closing up for the winter. There is a month before deer hunting season begins on November 1, but the water must be turned off, boats pulled up, docks secured, the cabins closed for the season and any foodstuffs to be saved put in the winter cellar.

The only reason the camps are opened for the deer season

is because Gary and Floyd love to hunt. There also is a crowd of about 25 regular hunters who are similarly afflicted and they are accommodated willingly. It lasts for two weeks and then the water is turned off for good.

In the old days the final job was to make a sign reading *This camp is not locked* and place it on a cabin that had been well stocked with wood, blankets and directions to the winter cellar where leftover canned goods were stored. This was in case a trapper or timber cruiser became stranded. Often the cabin would be used. Nowadays with snowmobilers knowing enough to travel in groups, there are fewer emergencies.

Both Cobb couples have spent winters in camp. Floyd and Maude went in the last day of December one year with two snowmobiles and a dog sled of supplies. To make matters even more exciting Maude had never driven one of the machines. The snow was deep and the close calls numerous. For fear that the ice was not thick enough Floyd elected to go from Lindsay Cove to the camp via the shore line and this trail was rough, causing several upsets. Each time they stopped they had to struggle against waist-deep snow. They eventually made it and as Maude recalls the situation:

"We did not celebrate New Year's Eve with Guy Lombardo."

Despite very cold weather and back troubles for Floyd, things straightened out and they began to enjoy themselves. They were snug and warm in the log cabin with the winter kitchen and they soon began to be visited by friends. The Haskells, Arthur and Yvette, from Long Falls Dam came in regularly with the mail and eventually a series of day trips were taken with the Haskells as well as with the Webbers, Phil and Phyllis. They covered the Dead River and Grand Falls areas, as well as Flagstaff Lake and all of the small ponds, High, Helen, the Otters, and the Carrys. Each noon they would have a cookout with venison burgers a feature. They got lost, which was part of the fun, but always managed to get home by dark.

To sum the winter up, Maude quoted a friend who said of an experience:

"Had a great time; wouldn't trade it for a million dollars, but also wouldn't do it again for another million."

Before the early 1960's, getting to camp in winter required snowshoes. The trip was made from the hatchery at Black Brook along an old, overgrown tote road at the base of Pierce Pond Mountain. Breaking that trail was tough duty, according to Gary, who said it was the most strenuous work he ever tackled.

When Floyd first had the camps, he would spend the winter lumbering in order to pay off the mortgage. In like manner, Gary has also worked in the woods. He and Greg Drummond have bought stumpage and cut as much as 100,000 board feet of pine. They also have cut 400-500 cords of pulp wood. Nowadays Greg and his wife Pat run a lodge for the benefit of skiers, skidoers and hunters, and Gary and Betty sneak off to Florida for a short break.

Fish Chowder

There are two secrets to a good fish chowder which most recipes overlook: use a tasty stock for the liquid and let the chowder season overnight. Others like to add some clam juice and chopped clams and Fanny Farmer, back in 1937, recommended soaking Boston crackers in cold milk before adding them as a final touch. Another wrinkle is to dice and dry out the salt pork so it can be used as a topping on the final product.

But no matter which variation you apply, somebody is bound to have a better idea. Discussing recipes can lead to blows and well may have done so long before this. The subject did sever one friendship at Pierce Pond, between Al Blake and Bill Hyer of Ridgefield, CT. They, along with Charlie Reiche, went to Mayor's Island for lunch one day and Al, who fancied himself as a chef, volunteered to make a fish chowder. Al had learned how to do it from Iral Bean, who may have gotten his recipe from Ma Sterling for whom he had guided in days past. Iral Bean is one of Pierce Pond's patron saints and is ranked with Arthur Macdougall's Dud Dean and Moscow's Rance Ham.

Al Blake was one of the lawyers from the Boston area who

came to Pierce Pond with the likes of Sherman Saltmarsh, who always took two days after landing in camp to get ready to fish. In this instance it is reported that Al took three hours to prepare his chowder. To keep his customers sullen, but not mutinous, he, or someone, had supplied a flask of Scotch, a snake bite medicine one uses before being bitten as well as after. In any event the chowder was finally completed, served and decorated with whatever accessories were available. Bill Hyer took a few mouthsful and laid his spoon down. Al was quick to notice.

"What's the matter, don't you like my chowder?"

"Too damn greasy," was Bill's comment and that started an argument that was never settled even unto death.

Guides have been making fish chowder as long as anyone can remember. It makes sense. Fish is readily available; any camp worth its bill always has potatoes, salt pork and onions on hand; and in the old days, before conservation became important, a chowder was as good a way to conceal the number of fish in camp as one could devise.

Fish chowder can be important to a guide. The way to a sport's pocketbook is through his stomach and the guide who can whip up a tasty meal is the more highly prized and rewarded. Thus, recipes are a topic of conversation at the guides' table in the kitchen along with women, fishing, women and the next trip to town.

Hugh Comber of Pleasant Pond was deemed to be the champion chowder maker of Pierce Pond during his era, which stretched over several administrations and ended in the Floyd-Maude years. When Gary came on board as a guide Hugh felt it was his duty to teach the young man how to make a chowder.

Accordingly one night at bedtime he began explaining how one fried out the salt pork, cooked the onions in the grease until just so, etc. Gary had to fight off sleep and managed to get in a "yup" or two in the right places. Had Hugh been less precise about his recipe, Gary might have lasted to hear the finale, but sleep finally took over as the milk was being added. As Gary tells the story, it was a good thing there was no quiz in the morning.

Arguments about chowder do last overnight as attested by Greg Drummond who had to listen to Lester Arsenault of North New Portland and Reggie McCollor of Bingham debate the subject far into the night. Greg was also in the kitchen the next morning when Lester came in, saw Reggie and said:

"Now, Reggie, when you were telling them boys how to make chowder, you didn't say about the onions. You *do* brown your onions, don't you?"

It was akin to drinking water after a night of champagne.

The guides also discuss the delicacies of cooking onions; some advocate boiling, others baking, and still others frying or creaming. Of late years the matter has reached a point where the guides are given a special opportunity to show their skills. Once a summer a cookout is held in the Wilderness Bound area and the guides put on an Onion Festival, cooking on open fires so all may see and then taste. The event has not developed to the point of awarding blue and red ribbons, like a state fair, but that is an idea. If Bob Witbeck were the judge, he would award one such to Gary Cobb for actually baking a loaf of bread for a noon meal, another to Greg Drummond for getting the most out of three chunks of cedar, including rinse water, and to Lester Arsenault for his mashed potatoes.

Fish chowder is also honored, once each week at Sunday noon, and while it is good, it is unlike the olden days when trout, salmon and pickerel were used. Today Betty Cobb gets fresh haddock, thus helping to conserve the local products.

The menu at camp has changed considerably since the early years, primarily because of the automobile which enables the camp owner to stay in closer touch with the outside. There was a time when the camp operator went into the woods to stay, more or less. Now it is nothing to go to North New Portland for supplies. This is why Betty Cobb is able to get fresh haddock for her chowders and even lobster for what has become the traditional fare for Friday dinner.

Back when the woods were being lumbered, camps fed their crews on such non-perishable foods as baked beans, potatoes, onions, and anything that could be made from flour, sugar and molasses. Any meat that was served came from the forest itself or had been smoked or salted previously. Vegetables included beans and more beans. Many a lumberman who saw a better future as a camp operator, such as Floyd Cobb, transferred the lumber camp fare, the only kind he knew, to his sporting camp. As Maude gained experience and transportation improved, so did camp menus.

As time went on and the state became more concerned with conservation, lumber camps as well as sporting camps were restricted as to the amount of fish and game they could consume. Today's emphasis on catch and release is 180 degrees apart from the original practices of woodsmen. And today's guest at a sporting camp does as well in camp as he might in town, if not better.

When camp operators were forced to eliminate fresh water fish and local game from their menus, their wives were driven to compensate with items equally attractive. This accounts for the importation of lobster once a week as well as fish chowder made from fresh haddock. Actually, chowder experts agree that chowder made from salt water fish has more distinction than that made from the fresh water variety, Ma Sterling to the contrary notwithstanding. One reason given is that haddock, for example, is firmer than trout or salmon and hence holds together better even as it flakes.

One holdover from the "good old days" is homemade bread and pastries. Pies at Pierce Pond continue to uphold the New England tradition of what dessert for hungry men should be. The bear that took the banana cake from the sideboard at Pierce Pond probably would have preferred apple pie, given his druthers, or better yet, blueberry pie in season (July). But homemade bread has an even greater hold on citified sports. Since the bulk of domestic buying is done these days at supermarkets, the chance of getting a good loaf of bread is thin, unless one has the time and patience to go out of one's way to find a bakery that caters to the more fastidious. Guests coming to Pierce Pond can look forward to large, thick slices of the stuff grandmother used to make, which is just as good, if not better, as toast or French toast, or even bread pudding—something else the average citizen never sees these days.

To support this baking binge the Cobbs estimate that they use 10,000 eggs a year and a ton and a half of flour. In addition to the pies, the flour goes into a dozen loaves of bread each day and that requires someone to get up early, like five o'clock.

Another reason for sporting camps to emphasize food is the cruel fact that fish do not bite on schedule, the weather is not always cooperative and most game is aware when the law is off them. Homemade soup not only helps to cure colds, it also helps to assuage the blues.

It was not always thus. In the early years of the first Cobb administration, a doctored up version of clam chowder was served on Friday nights. The base was Snow's Clam Chowder, but Maude knew that seafood chowders needed to cure awhile and that certain spices help the process. In fact, she did such a good job that one guest asked Sarah Arsenault, the waitress, if the chowder were homemade. She said "yes," and went about her business. All might have been well, had not the guest then asked for the recipe. Sarah burst into the kitchen with:

"Now we really are in trouble," and explained her gaffe. A council of war was held in the kitchen and a recipe was devised on the basis of how those involved would attempt to make a clam chowder from scratch. Which gets us back to Betty Cobb insisting that fresh haddock be had for the fish chowder she now serves regularly.

The recipe for pancakes goes back to Doris Grieve who experimented over the years. The one for oatmeal bread is also old. It was created by Trudy Gilbert who, along with her husband guide Bruce Gilbert, worked for the Grieves.

Unlike most restaurateurs, the Cobbs willingly give out their recipes. For one thing they are friendly and warm-hearted folk and for another, a stack of Pierce Pond pancakes served in someone's home only reminds that someone of where he or she got the idea in the first place.

Neighbors

When one visits Pierce Pond Camps, takes the short boat ride from Lindsay Cove, and finally lands at the dock, the impression received is one of isolation. And if one is able to fly over the pond that impression is strengthened even more. Scarcely a roof is to be seen for miles. But there are neighbors, even though all of them cannot be seen.

For example, Central Maine Power Company maintains caretakers at Long Falls Dam, which lies eight miles north of Pierce Pond on the Dead River. From 1963 to 1979, Arthur and Yvette Haskell were stationed there and proved more than friends to two generations of Cobbs. In spring and winter, the Cobbs would use the Haskell house as a jumping off place for trips into the camps. Snowmobiles were stored there and on occasion overnight stays were made. Gary and Arthur have trapped together.

Part of the job of dam caretaker is to measure snowfall for both the weather bureau and for Central Maine Power. The peak during the Haskell regime was 238 inches in 1968-69. That's two inches shy of 20 feet. In fact, during that same winter they were isolated for eleven days by a six-foot blizzard.

Long Falls Dam was created to form Flagstaff Lake and

until 1975, the dam caretakers had to be alert for the spring drive of logs which saw large rafts of pulpwood, some 2,000 cords per raft, towed the length of the lake and then sluiced through the gates of the dam and down the river to the mills. On one such occasion Arthur Haskell got word to close down the gates as a riverman had fallen from his bateau. The body of Jim Dyer of Highland was recovered near Caratunk, some 20 miles down river.

It says something about the Haskells when it is noted that since they retired to Embden in 1979, there have been four caretakers on the job. Apparently it is not as easy as it may sound.

Of equal importance over the years have been the people at the Dead River Hatchery on Black Brook. One gets to the hatchery by taking the first road to the left after leaving the tarred highway from North New Portland. The state built and operated the hatchery for 20 years until 1965. The Schoen-thaler family of Waterville assumed ownership of the hatchery and hired Deb Sylvester, an old trapper, as a caretaker. He and Gary became quite friendly as their traplines crossed. Deb, whose family at one time ran the King and Bartlett Camps, knew a good doughnut when he smelled one and got into the habit of visiting Pierce Pond Camps when Betty was likely to have some on hand, which is most of the time.

The value of good neighbors was proved in 1965, when Gary, driving into camp one winter's day from Bingham, hit an icy spot and found himself about as close to members of his family as he had ever been. The truck hit a snow bank, was flipped over onto its roof and ended up crossways to the road.

Fortunately, there were four people and a dog scrunched together in the cab, so that no one was injured. Gary hiked back to the Scott Paper Company Camp at Carrying Place where he found a French cook who was able to call Joe Thibodeau, the manager of the hatchery at Black Brook. Thibodeau and the Scott woods foreman got the truck back on its wheels and running. It was decided to spend the night at the gate camp.

Gary hiked into camp to raid the winter cellar for beans and soup and almost paid too much for them. On his return he kept falling asleep and only made it out to the gate through sheer determination.

The next day Joe Thibodeau helped get the truck started again and Gary, Betty, his sister Judy and her boyfriend began the trip back. It was devilishly cold without windshield, windows and heater, so Gary left the others with Iral Bean at Bingham and continued on alone to Lee, a matter of some four hours.

Evelyn and Phil Sawyer now run the hatchery, and specialize in shipping salmon to the west coast for direct consumption by individuals, but the trapping business has slowed up. Elden and Laurie McLean of Embden still carry on the tradition, but two winter shelters, evidence of a trapper's way of life, have finally disappeared. These were made of cedar logs, about four feet high, with no floors or windows, just enough to get a trapper out of the weather for a night. One was at Black Brook and the other near the Upper Pond.

Another lumber camp site that is now converted to other purposes is the area around the gate. In addition to the gate camp itself there is another cabin nearby owned by Albert Martin, a seasonal resident since 1947. In that year, Albert and his brother-in-law, Maurice Michaud of Lexington, took over an old lumber camp cabin that had been used during the 30's and 40's. In essence, they squatted. Eight years later the cabin burned and Albert rebuilt on the spot and the Scott Paper Company granted him a lease.

Albert Martin is an unusual man. He came from a large Canadian family and was born on Lac Megantic. With such a limited beginning and having spent his life in the woods, Albert might be expected to have a limited education. Not so. He can speak three languages, can overhaul a diesel motor and is well read, especially in ancient history. He makes good company for the gatekeeper and has come to know a number of camp guests.

Directly across the pond from the campgrounds is a boat house and higher up the remains of a large house. The latter is an example of what can happen when lightning strikes in the woods. The house was built in 1919 by George Spalding of Caratunk for Louis Smith of Holliston, MA. Smith was a guest at Pierce Pond Camps during Armond Spalding's regime, 1916-1921, and the two locked horns. Smith vowed he would build his own place in a prominent spot that Armond would have to look at the rest of his life.

Smith managed to get a lease from Great Northern Paper Company, despite Armond Spalding's efforts to the contrary, and he put up a boat house in which the crew lived until the main house, up on the cliff above, was finished. It was a handsome affair, some 50 feet in length, complete with a stone fireplace. It is said that Ben Ames Williams used the spot as the location for his novel, *Leave Her To Heaven*, which later was made into a successful movie. Williams came to Pierce Pond to escape civilization, was enchanted by the Smith abode and incorporated the site in his book. He may have also been impressed by the fact that Smith used one guide to make a trip daily to Caratunk for fresh dairy products.

In the 1940's Smith willed his place to Charles Williams, a fellow Hollistonian. Charlie used it three or four times a year and called upon Pierce Pond Camps to provide ferry service. Then in 1967 came the bolt of lightning and despite the efforts of Floyd Cobb and Richard Cobb, the building was completely decimated. Only the stone fireplace remains. The boathouse has since been converted to a cabin. Charlie Williams, now in his 90's, turned over the ownership and lease to Gary Cobb, who maintains the place for a few of Charlie's friends who visit in the summer.

Armond Spalding was still alive when the fire occurred and felt that a bit of justice had prevailed.

The only wooded island in Lower Pierce Pond has been called Iral's Island, Holbrook Island and now Abbe's Island. The setting is picturesque which no doubt is why a Harry Holbrook and a Dr. Knowlton arranged for a lease of the land from Great Northern Paper Company in 1910. They then had Charles Spalding build the present camp. That explains the name Holbrook and when one learns that Iral Bean was caretaker of the island for many years, it is easily understood why it was called his island at times. In due course the island was handed down to the Abbe family, which has since purchased it.

The Guides

The designation, Maine guide, evokes visions of hardy woodsmen who are in command of every situation, who are looked up to by king and tycoon alike, and who view the wilds of Maine as their own private property. Yet to document their exalted status takes more than mere scholarship. Maine guides are an elusive breed. One can find brief references to W. W. Sewall of Hook Point Camps at Island Falls because he chanced to hob nob with President Theodore Roosevelt, who loved publicity, but for the most part guides get only minor and local notice.

The one Maine guide who had volumes devoted to his activities was Dud Dean and he was the product of the fertile imagination of Arthur Macdougall, Jr., the Bingham cleric who would seem to have made a better living telling stories than preaching the Gospel. According to Nellie Macdougall Parks of Bingham, the Reverend's daughter, Dud Dean was a composite of a number of guides of the Upper Kennebec region. The Dud may have come from Dud Preble, but the one who influenced him the most was Jack Owens, a neighbor. Owens was the one who got Macdougall interested in fishing, gave him his first fly rod, and became a "father figure" for Macdougall, a relationship that the latter had missed when he was growing up.

The two Bingham families became so close that the Macdougall tribe came to call Jack "Daddy Owens." The latter had many of the characteristics that were to be given to Dud Dean, who was portrayed as soft spoken, full of humor and a great storyteller. The stories intrigued Macdougall in particular and he would often drop in to see Owens and the two would smoke their dudeens, short Irish pipes, and trade stories. The word *dudeen* and the name "Dud Dean" are too close to be coincidental. Since Owens had associated with the other guides in the area, Dud Preble, Rance Ham, John Morris, the Spaldings, the Beans, and the many Durgins of The Forks, it can easily be imagined that their stories as well as those of Owens himself were aired and stored for future use in the pages of *Field and Stream* and other publications. It is still disturbing that less is known about Preble, Ham, Owens *et al* than about Dud Dean, the fictional guide.

We do know a bit about Ham. He was from Moscow and came into prominence when he caught a 16-pound salmon at Pierce Pond in 1903. From correspondence it is known that his business picked up considerably after that for he guided out of East Carry Pond as well as Otter Pond. It is also known that Henry J. Lane, who was Ham's boss at East Carry Pond, planned to put cabins on Pierce Pond so that his guests could take advantage of the excellent fishing there.

Although he did his best to hide his name of Rancelear, it is understandable how Rance Ham came by it. His mother, who was a Quint of New Portland, led a dramatic life in her youth and well may be excused for such flights of fancy. Her parents drove a herd of cattle from Embden to Canada via the Canada Road in 1820 and settled there. Shortly thereafter an epidemic broke out, and, fearing for the lives of their children, the Quints made arrangements with an Indian to have the children returned to Embden. Their foresight paid off and the Quint son and daughter were brought back to this country. The daughter later became Rance Ham's mother. There are several granddaughters still living along the Kennebec, including Marsha Crombie of Bingham who supplied the story of the trip to Canada.

Back in 1897 the Maine Fish Commission made a survey of the other occupations of registered Maine guides and came up with a list of 83 such jobs, ranging from one pension attorney to one combined musician and barber. The rest of the list is equally intriguing:

> 12 boat and canoe makers, 2 keeper of boats, 1 bush whacker, 5 barbers, 17 maker of canoes, snow shoes and Indian wares, 1 bottoming chairs, 1 bleacher, 1 blacksmith, 1 boarding house proprietor, 2 butchers, 2 bookkeepers, 42 cooks, 30 carpenters, 1 cashier in sand bank, 8 clerks, 1 cobbler, 132 common laborers, 21 camp proprietors, 1 carder and spinner, 2 carriage manufacturers, 1 civil engineer and land agent, 1 log cabin builder, 1 cook and carpenter, 1 druggist, 1 dealer in carriages, 1 dam and pier builder, 1 deep sea fisherman, 1 express agent, 1 excelsior maker, 1 engineer, 1 fireman, 1 fur hunter, 3 game wardens, 18 hunters, 1 harness maker and repairer, 1 hostler, 3 hotel proprietors, 281 farmers, 7 Jack-at-all trades,

2 jewelers, 74 lumberers, 9 merchants, 2 machinists, 1 mechanic, 16 millmen, 2 mechanical engineers, 2 mail carriers, 1 metal sealer, 1 maker of snow shoes and moccasins, 3 painters, 1 painter and paper hanger, 1 professional loafer, 1 postal clerk, 1 pounder of hooks in logs, 1 paper maker, 2 railroad tie makers, 42 river drivers, 2 reporters, 10 surveyors, 1 scaler, 8 spool makers, 2 students, 5 spruce gum pickers, 8 steamboat proprietors, 1 stage driver, 1 superintendent of lumber operations, 10 taxidermists, 9 teamsters, 27 trappers, 1 time scaler, 1 tax collector, 1 teacher, 1 tanner, 1 town official and trial justice, 35 woodsmen, 1 wood turner, 1 camp proprietor and farmer, 1 farmer and postmaster, 1 stevedore, 1 railroadman, 2 farmer and stone-mason, 1 plumber and bookkeeper, 1 roofer, 1 proprietor of billiard and pool room, 1 dam caretaker at South Twin Dam.

It is not surprising to see that farmers, river drivers, trappers, lumberers and woodsmen bulk the list of occupations. Traditionally, Maine guides were men who lived in the wilds and knew where fish and game were to be found. In their spare time they would reveal some of their secrets for a little hard cash.

Of the present guides at Pierce Pond, Greg Drummond runs a lodge for hunters, skiers and snowmobilers and also cuts wood during the off season. Dave Peppard is a game warden, Steve Staples is a commercial bait trapper and dealer, Chris Leo is a surveyor, Bill Howe manages a wood turning mill, Paul Pono is a jack-of-all trades, Mark Goodwin builds canoes and

Shane Nichols and Andy Cobb are in college, one aiming to be a game warden and the other the next proprietor of Pierce Pond Camps.

Another reason for the want of documentary evidence about guides is that few, if any, have the inclination to put their experiences on paper. Nor, for that matter, do their customers. Fishermen will write of their triumphs, but they prefer to take any credit due, rather than to bestow it. An exception to this rule was Henry David Thoreau who secured a place in history for Joe Polis, his Indian guide, by including him in his book about the Maine woods. A lesser known writer, Dr. Augustus C. Hamlin of Bangor, gave great credit to his Indian guide, Peol Toma, who introduced Hamlin to the landlocked salmon of Grand Lake Stream.

Otherwise the fame of Maine guides is known primarily to the patrons of those camps from which the individual guides operate. There is a great bond between most guides and their sports. No matter how famous or successful a sport may be in his own territory, he is just another customer when out in a guide's canoe. In some instances the bond becomes a solid one, as witness the affection that Gary Cobb had for Erastus Corning II, the long-time mayor of Albany, NY. In fact, assigning guides is one of the headaches a camp owner has to endure. Too many patrons want the same guide at the same time.

This is not to say that all guides are of heroic stature. Take Greg Drummond, for example, who admitted he knew very little about fishing when he started out. In fact, on his first trip he advised his sport of this fact and thus agreed to let the sport make all of the decisions. Accordingly he was taken to the Basin on the east side of Pierce Pond and was told to follow the shoreline closely in order to get a lure close to a certain spot that the sport knew to be productive. Greg did as he was told and promptly beached the craft. Things have gone much better for Greg, now that he is well seasoned, knowledgeable and popular.

One sport to whom Greg Drummond became attached was Granville Bond of Bangor, a grain salesman who fished all over the state and was well known and popular. At age 85, which puts the date at 1985 for he was born at the turn of the century, he had to be helped over rough spots and in one instance didn't make it, falling into a brook despite assistance fore and aft. Greg was more upset than Granville, who promptly took off all of his clothes, except shoes, hat and shorts, and hung the rest on some bushes to dry. He explained that this was not the first time he had got wet in the woods. He made quite a sight, according to Greg, what with an expansive middle which was well scarred from numerous operations. Granville did not consider the situation unusual and went about his business as though nothing had happened.

A year or two later, Granville confessed to Greg that despite all of his experience, he had never caught a trophy trout and had set such an occurrence as a final goal. Accordingly Greg suggested that they go to Upper Kilgore Pond which had been producing some sizeable fish. They got an early start and they fished all day without a sign of a trout. Come the afternoon, about 5 p.m. Granville asked Greg if he would get into trouble if he were late getting back to camp. Greg responded in the negative, whereupon Granville replied:

"I'd like to fish through the evening hours. I figure I'll

never get up here again."

So they kept on fishing and as often is the case, the fish began to move. Just as Greg was maneuvering the canoe to get into a better position, Granville spotted a rise and flicked his fly onto the target. The combined action of the turning canoe and Granville's cast caused an awkward situation. Granville hooked the fish with his back to it. It was a good fish and well could have solved his problem, but the fish was not hooked properly and soon broke off. Again Greg made a move. This time he placed his anchor near shore behind some weeds so that Granville could cast out beyond where bugs were working. This proved a good move, except that there's nothing a trout likes better than a patch of weeds into which to drive once hooked. Twice Granville hooked hefty trout and twice the fish entangled themselves in the weeds.

The fourth trout showed good sense and moved into deep water. Greg advised Granville to ease out some line so he, Greg, could move back and pull up the anchor. Once that maneuver was made, they were then in a good position to play the trout. But the trout did not want to play. He hung on the bottom and refused to come up, no matter how hard Granville tried to move him. Eventually the hook came loose and once again Granville was defeated. By this time darkness had set in and the pair reluctantly headed back to camp.

During the winter Granville died and in the spring of 1989 his son Norris, who had long before been introduced to Pierce Pond, came for his annual trip. He decided that he and Greg should go to Kilgore if for no other reason than pure sentiment. As might be expected Norris hooked a five-pound trout. It was good enough to take top honors for the season. What was not expected was that as the two men gazed at the beauty as it lay in the net, tears came to both of them.

Dave Pooler, the Bingham guide, was involved in a similar search for a hefty trout and did it voluntarily. Two guests, one a boisterous boor and the other a gentle professor, got into a torrid discussion of the virtues of bait fishing versus the use of flies. Each proclaimed that his method was guaranteed to produce the bigger fish. The vigor of the argument can be measured by the size of the bet placed–$100. Dave overheard all this and since he was free and also prejudiced in favor of the professor, he offered his services without charge. He, too, suggested Kilgore as the venue for the fly fishing test. Accordingly, they headed in that direction with the assumption they would be back the same day. Unfortunately, the trout in Kilgore refused to cooperate. A whole day went by and even though they had not provisioned themselves for an extended stay, stay they did, to the delight of the no-see-ums.

The situation did not improve on the second day, but Dave had faith in the pond and the professor had faith in Dave, so they continued fishing on the third day. Finally, that afternoon their determination was rewarded. A big rise, the right fly and a good cast produced a most handsome fish.

The return to camp attracted much attention. After all, they had been AWOL for two nights and everyone in camp was aware why. Heading the reception committee was the bait fisherman who had previously dredged a six-pounder from the bottom of the Lower Pond. He was anxious to collect his $100. Dave and the professor showed no emotion and said nothing.

Dave unloaded his canoe and the professor walked slowly to his cabin, which indicated to the bait fisherman, at least, that he had won the bet. He began to gloat, but to make certain of his victory, he checked Dave's canoe. There lying across several ribs was the professor's eight-and-a-half-pound beauty.

The dean of guides at Pierce Pond in the first half of the present century was Iral Bean of Caratunk. He began as a teenager under Armond Spalding and continued on under the Mitchells, Harrimans, Grieves and Cobbs. He also guided out of the Sterling and Otter Pond Camps. In short, Iral Bean knew as much about the Pierce Pond area as anyone before him or since, and he would be the first to admit it. He had an immediate answer for every question and the questions came often to him since he really did know most of the answers. He was especially canny about where and when fish might be expected to rise.

Iral was the epitome of the Maine guide. He had big hands and long arms, and could hoist a pack with the best of them, despite a limp caused by a woods accident. He was in control at all times except when he was guiding Mrs. Virginia Kennie from Scarsdale, NY. She was his Achilles' heel. She and her husband George had control of a water company in New York City and it is entirely possible that her aristocratic manner was more than Iral Bean could handle. No one else ever made him boil the silverware before each noon cook-out and no one else insisted on a clean tablecloth each day. This was a species that Iral was not familiar with and he took his cue from husband George who rarely said anything. So while the Kennies were in camp, usually two or three weeks at a time, Iral earned his money, particularly since Mrs. Kennie insisted that they troll and that Iral should row the Sponson steadily.

Since sports pay the freight, they can and do, make demands, such as fancy meals cooked out in the woods. Mr. and Mrs. Sam Breed of Swampscott, MA had definite ideas as to what they would eat and who would cook it. Sam Breed had been introduced to the area by his father-in-law, William Beardsell of Philadelphia, and at one time was part owner of Otter Pond Camps. Whenever the Breeds came to fish, Mr. Breed insisted that Iral Bean be his guide and Mrs. Breed, equally determined, asked for Bert Morris. Bert was known as the best dressed guide in the business and came to work in starched shirt and suit.

With the Breeds, the noon meal was a three-hour production calling for trout, salmon and partridge. This was not unusual in those days, but a generation gap developed when Louise Breed married Doug Allen. Doug, it must be pointed out, is the son of Clarence Allen, the founder of Camp Chewonki near Wiscasset, which puts great emphasis on nature, conservation and similar points of view. On Doug's first trip out with the Breeds at Pierce Pond, he was apprehensive. For one thing both Iral Bean and Bert Morris carried fire-arms and as soon as they pitched camp for the noon meal, they disappeared into the woods. In due course they returned with several grouse.

How, Doug Allen wanted to know, had these birds been obtained? After all, he had been influenced by Roger Tory Peterson, the famous naturalist, at Camp Chewonki.

Both Iral and Bert were quick to assure him, if not convince him, that the birds had died of natural causes.

The majority of guides who have been associated with

Pierce Pond have come from the towns along the Kennebec such as Bingham, Caratunk, The Forks and Moscow, although a few have hailed from as far west as Dixfield and as far to the east as Lee. Over the nearly 100 years since a camp has been on the pond, a sort of fraternity has developed that causes natives living along the river to boast of the fact that their fathers and grandfathers guided out of Pierce Pond. Iral Bean, for example, had four brothers, Carl, Earl, Oral and Ural as well as two sons, Eldon and Bunny, in the business. The Durgin family of The Forks was equally prominent in the field. Early in the present century, Ed, Frank and Ira Durgin began the family tradition and later it was carried on by Walter in the 1920's and by Sturgis in the 40's.

Carl Bean died with his boots on even though he was sitting in a camp kitchen at the time. Seems that he was guiding at the Norways, a section north of Pierce Pond where Spencer Stream enters the Dead River. He had just returned from a day in the woods, had taken a seat in the kitchen and was about to regale Tom Bigelow, the cook, with the details of his day. When Bigelow lit a lamp, trouble descended. The lamp caused a reflection to bounce from a hanging pan out a window. Carl's sport, not realizing he was so close to camp, mistook the reflection for a deer's eyes and fired. His aim was true, and fatal. Carl was killed instantly, shot through the head.

The coroner was brought in and eventually the body was taken out on a travois, the Indian sledge that is dragged behind a horse. The hunting party went out with the body and on the rough journey the rifle owned by the same sport who had killed Carl went off accidently and struck Harry Pooler, the teamster, in the arm. The horse bolted as a final indignity.

Guy Bean, Carl's cousin, also was shot by a hunter. Guy was mistaken for a bear near the trail leading from the river to the Otter Ponds. Guy, fortunately, survived despite the fact that the 35-caliber bullet pierced both of his lungs.

Paul Meservey of Caratunk recalls that his grandfather, Lee, of Indian descent, guided for the Spaldings while living on, or close to, the original Pierce property on the Kennebec. Lee later worked as a cook for Great Northern Paper Company in the various company camps in the area, and in 1916, along with his son Elmon, volunteered for the Mexican War. It seemed fitting that a man who had cooked as a guide in lumber camps wound up doing the same thing while his buddies were chasing Pancho Villa.

While every guide varies in personality and competence just as ordinary citizens do, some stand out in memory more than others. For example, Alfred Marble of East Peru was noted for his repartee and is fondly recalled by sports, guides and camp operators. He was eager and boisterous and often in trouble, such as the time Alys Eastman of Fryeburg fell overboard while trying to step into a canoe and Alfred, in his haste to come to her rescue, did likewise. He also was known for his frenetic pace and his fondness for his deteriorating Rambler car. On one occasion Floyd called him to guide a guest and Alfred, rushing to accommodate his boss, drove his car all the way to the beach at Lindsay Cove. As soon as he stepped out of the vehicle to greet Floyd, the two front wheels dropped off.

"Some car," commented Floyd.

"Well, I tell you," responded Alfred, "that car is so eager

to go I've had to resort to removing the wheels to keep it in place."

Alfred Marble figured in another episode that still gets talked about when the subject of guides gets brought up at Pierce Pond. Items of this genre usually involve guests as well since some guests can be rated as "characters" as can some guides. The guests featured in this story werre from Boston, one weighing about 400 pounds and the other a crusty colonel who never forgot he got to be one. Neither of these fishermen could be labelled as "kinder and gentler" as the term is applied today and, in fact, the atmosphere in the guides' camp was more than calm when the matter of which guides were going to have to put up with which of these guest was discussed. On the morning under discussion, Hugh Comber had drawn the big man and Iral Bean, the colonel.

Comber declared that he was not going to risk his canoe with such a heavy guest and demanded that a solid rowboat be prepared. When the guest was asked to step into it, he balked. There was an awkward pause, but when Hugh Comber explained that his canoe was in the shop for repairs, the guest grudgingly relented and stepped into the boat. He not only stepped into it, but through it as well. The sudden giving of the floor boards caused the guest to fall back on the seat, which also surrendered. As the rowboat slowly began to sink in view of the usual morning crowd on the dock, Alfred Marble put his hand on Hugh Comber's shoulder and whispered:

"There goes your tip for today, Hughie."

Just at that moment, the Colonel appeared. He had a bad leg and used a cane for support. He marched out onto the dock, ignoring what was going on, and headed right for Iral Bean, who was to be his guide. Waving a book of flies in Iral's face, he demanded:

"Does it make any difference which fly I use?"

"Not to me it don't," replied Iral.

One guide helped Floyd Cobb wage war on a redundance of raccoons. Being of a charitable nature, Floyd omits the name of the guide involved when he tells the story. It seems that a preponderance of *Procyon lotor* forced Floyd to take action against the critters, so one night he and said guide headed for the camp dump with a flashlight and two .22 caliber pistols. As soon as they turned on the torch they found themselves surrounded by numerous pairs of eyes. At once they began firing and literally shot the lights out. When they had finished they swept the area with the light and found to their amazement that they not only had killed a number of raccoons, but three black bear as well.

The guide, who did most of the talking about the exploit, remained a hero for only 24 hours. The next night a noise on the kitchen roof indicated that not all of the ring-tails had been eliminated. Our hero immediately stepped into the breach and emptied his revolver at the critter from 20 feet away. It barely batted an eye and went on about its business.

On the other hand, two more reliable guides, Oscar Jones and Bert Morris, created the "Sulking Ring," a device guaranteed most instances) to move sulking salmon off the bottom. Big fish still have a tendency to seek the bottom in self-defense, as as seen in Granville Bond's unsuccessful effort in the Upper Pond. Jones was the inventor of the ring and Bert Morris, a part-time blacksmith, the manufacturer. They had seen the need for action and came up with an iron ring, about 2 1/2 inches in diameter, that could be snapped around a taut line. The ring then would slide down the line until it hit the salmon's nose, thereby causing the fish to think about moving. The device was successful on its maiden voyage to the deep, thus enabling Dr. A. K. Coomar-Swamy, a curator at the Boston Museum of Fine Arts, to land an 11-pounder, which was of sufficient caliber to cause comment in the *Boston Herald.*

Perhaps the best-known Maine guide was the first one ever registered. That she was a woman also made her that much more newsworthy. Cornelia T. "Flyrod" Crosby was born at Phillips in 1854 and spent her life fishing and hunting in Maine. A natural athlete, she also was natural copy for newspapermen as well as a natural promoter in her own right. At the first national exhibition put on in 1895 by the New York Sportsman's Association in Madison Square Garden, Flyrod appeared in a green leather hunting suit, the skirt of which was a full seven inches off the floor. This led to questions about her dress and she revealed that she had never worn a corset nor did she resort to knickerbockers. Neither of these things had anything to do with hunting or fishing, but they did tend to liven up the story, which she, and the reporter interviewing her, well knew.

That she was the first registered guide came about because of her interest in the subject. She had been called to Augusta when a bill to license Maine guides was being discussed. She was in favor of the measure and when it was passed she was given the honor of receiving license number one. It is alleged that she was the last person to shoot a caribou in Maine legally, at Eagle Lake in 1898.

Another factor which extended her reputation was the company in which she traveled. The men behind the New York Sportsman's Show included J. Pierpont Morgan, August Belmont, Theodore Roosevelt, Grover Cleveland and the then Lieutenant Robert E. Peary. They dominated the rugged individualist movement and Flyrod fit into the picture gracefully and easily. She became the friend of Annie Oakley and the leading newspapers of the East opened their pages to her. They loved to hear about such accomplishments as catching, cleaning and cooking 52 trout in 42 minutes.

In the second national sportsman's show held in New York, Flyrod was in charge of the Maine exhibition and gave *The New York Times* a full preview of what she planned to bring to the city. Included was a log cabin, built near Bemis, and a stuffed moose, so large it had to be shipped in a special railroad car. It is not surprising to learn that Flyrod lived to be 93 years of age. Theodore Roosevelt (1858-1919) was the ring leader of the New York crowd, primarily because he sought and got considerable publicity as an outdoorsman. He came to Maine at 18 during his first Christmas vacation from Harvard. He went to Hook Point Camps at Island Falls and became so fond of W. W. Sewall, the camp owner, that he took Sewall and his nephew, Will Dood, out west to manage his ranch in the Dakotas. J. Pierpont Morgan also was fond of Maine and owned Spring Lake Camps near Flagstaff at one time.

According to Gary, who, after 33 years should know, the camaraderie among the guides is just as strong now as it was in

1958 when he first broke bread in the guides' kitchen. They kid among themselves, argue and subtly trade secrets. The only difference between the old days and the present is that the fishing is harder and guides have to know more than their predecessors did. To catch trophy-sized fish and keep sports happy is no mean trick these days. Fish are fewer and competition keener. It is necessary to be more observant and to know when to expect what flies to appear. Entemology plays a much greater role than it did in the days when landlocked salmon were first recognized and when a man could take 25 fish on 25 casts.

Guides are also good listeners, semi-psychologists in practice. Many a sport has unburdened himself of his problems to a guide. Fishermen relax in the company of a congenial guide and in many instances deep friendships are developed. After all, human nature has not changed that much in the last millenium.

And guides these days must have a greater concern for conservation. They are the ones who have made the "catch and release" program so successful. They operate on the theory that they will return every fish caught unless instructed otherwise by the sport. They also are proud to be operating out of Pierce Pond. They consider it an honor as do the natives in the area. Reggie McCollor, of Bingham, who guided at Pierce Pond after World War II, has said that the old timers "considered Pierce Pond a special place and always looked forward to going in there."

The Gatekeepers

Visitors to Pierce Pond Camps get a good first impression of the place when they reach the gate some two and a half miles from the pond itself. There they are greeted by a self-proclaimed "middle-aged" (78) former Maine woodsman with a cheerful smile and a twinkling eye. His name is Romeo St. John and he was born in St. John, Maine, way up on the Canadian border and he is about as fine an example of the old-time logger as one would want to meet.

His father was a woodsman, buying stumpage from land owners, organizing a crew of lumberjacks and spending the winter in the woods cutting timber. Once the trees were felled they were skidded to the nearest water in which they were floated to a saw mill come spring. When the logs, marked by the logger's special device, reached the mill, then and only then did the logger get paid for his efforts.

Romeo experienced every job in the lumbering business. He worked the Allagash and the St. John and he was a foreman on the last log drive on the Kennebec in 1975. He also was well known for his ability to handle a batteau and fought the fire that resulted from the Great Northern Paper Company's efforts to log the Pierce Pond area. The gate which Romeo now keeps was originated in 1951 when the company began its short-lived operations at Pierce Pond.

The original intent was to keep inquisitive people away from their lumbering operations and also to protect Pierce Pond Camps from any further intrusion caused by their activities. After the fire, when Great Northern decided to move out of the area, the gate and a portion of the land around it was leased to the camps, including rights to the full use of the road down to and including the cove. When Scott Paper Company obtained ownership of the land in 1955 such leases and rights were honored and still are.

For Pierce Pond Camps the gate is most useful. It provides a way for the camp to be notified of arriving guests so that they may be met by a boat. It also helps to protect the pond from abuse and overuse as well as providing protection for vehicles and other property left at Lindsay Cove. Finally, the gate serves as a screen for the general public, which is allowed to use the road for a minimal fee. The gatekeepers, being woodsmen for the most part, have been well prepared to handle the obstreperous.

In the beginning the company put one of its own men on the gate, but eventually it became the responsibility of the camp to man it. One of the first to get the job was Dave Pooler, a guide from across the Kennebec at Caratunk, whose career in the area goes back to the Spalding days. His name is mentioned in various reports of successful fishing and hunting expeditions in the media of the day, notably the *Maine Woods,* where in 1908 he is recorded as having guided a hunting party out of East Carry Pond Camps.

With one exception the gatekeepers during the Cobb years have all been retired woodsmen and definite Maineacs. As such they have made ideal official greeters for the camps. By and large they have been dependable, of good humor, forthright and loquacious. Men who have been holed up in the woods for months at a time tend to seek society when they get out and want to make the most of any contacts they have with people.

The one exception to the Maineac rule was Cliff Peck, who came from Niantic, CT and was on the gate in the early 1980's. He was a chicken farmer who came to Maine and caught fish fever, to the extent that he and his wife Ethel would drive all night from Connecticut, fish all day at Pierce Pond and then drive back all night. They had more energy than any two people who have ever trod the territory and when they retired they moved to Detroit, Maine, near Newport. Thus they were able to fish every day, even in the winter and as far away as the ocean.

The Pecks were talkers. If Cliff saw deer tracks on the beach, he would estimate there were 40,000 such tracks which amounted to 10,000 deer. Their vegetables, of which there were many, would always be the biggest and best of any for miles around. For proof, the Pecks would drive home, pick and can a mess of vegetables and return to Pierce Pond the same day. Since they were at Pierce Pond so much they learned quickly that Howard Monroe, who had been on the gate in 1977 died that year. They asked if they might have the job which would put them that much closer to their favorite fishing spots.

Cliff also was a guide which made him even more valuable

to the camps and so he and Ethel moved into the little cabin by the gate, which they promptly spruced up with a fence and a lawn. Unfortunately their tenure was all too short, for Cliff was killed by a railroad train in 1984. He was crossing the tracks in back of his son's house in Newport, when he was struck. His wife Ethel still comes back to visit.

To get back to the Maineacs, Claude Goodrich, from Bingham, was the first gatekeeper the Cobbs knew for he had taken over from Dave Pooler in the mid-1950's while the Grieves were in charge. He was in his 70's when he took the job. He had never owned or driven an automobile, had raised seven children and boasted of 22 grandchildren. His part in the lumber business was in the production end so that he knew wood and how to work it. During the long hours on the gate he would make jewelry boxes and cedar chests which he would give away. As with the other gatekeepers, Claude was a story-teller, a character, and something of a ham. He loved to show the claw marks made by a bear on his cabin to arriving guests, which, on second thought, really *is* something to talk about.

He was a descendent of one of the earliest pioneers in the Upper Kennebec Valley and liked to talk about the folks in that area. One of his favorites was about one of the Durgins going up to the pearly gates. The Durgins came from The Forks in large numbers. Some even guided in the Pierce Pond area. Apparently this member of the clan not only was rebuked by St. Peter in heaven, but later by Beelzebub below.

"Do you mean to say," he exclaimed when he got the bad news, "that I've got to go back to The Forks?"

Harry Allen succeeded Claude Goodrich at the gate for a

year and a half. He was another woodsman and came from Lee, the Cobb stamping ground. Harry was best known for his love of Narragansett beer and his fantasies. If Floyd or Gary would stop by the gate and Harry was feeling no pain, he might throw a stone into the bush. Asked why he had done that, he would reply:

"Gladys is in there and I want her to come out and meet you."

In 1967 he fell into the spring and broke his arm, opening the way for Howard Monroe, also from Lee. He had been a teamster, a woodsman, a river driver and well-known guide and still was a great storyteller. He used to talk about the time he got an owl without firing a shot. He was coming back to camp after using up all his ammunition when he spotted an owl looking at him. As he walked slowly by the tree in which the owl was perched, Howard noticed that the owl kept turning his head. So Howard decided to try an experiment. He began to circle the tree. The owl kept his eye on the man below and continued to turn his head. Howard kept going and the third time around the tree he heard a snap and the owl fell to the ground at his feet.

Like Claude Goodrich, Howard Monroe did not drive and as a consequence saw more of the Cobbs, father and son, than the other gatekeepers. He was a small man, with thick glasses and a caricature for a face, but the children loved him and he loved them. He always had some candies or other goodies tucked away for their pleasure. He also liked to go to the Skowhegan Fair and Floyd and Maude not only took him one time, but also treated him to a fancy dinner at the Candlelight

Restaurant. When his dinner was served, Howard reached for the salt and because of the dim light and his poor eyesight he had a hard time managing. He banged the salt cellar on the table, arousing everyone's attention, and still did not think he was getting any results. Finally he complained in a loud voice to Floyd:

"There ain't no goddam salt in this thing, is there Floyd?"

Another time Gary and Betty took him to a doctor when they were living at Millinocket. The waiting room was crowded and the wait was long. Finally, Howard couldn't contain himself.

"By God," he exclaimed, "I'm likely to die before I get to see that doctor."

Howard Monroe represented a generation of Mainers which knew life in the raw. Living in the woods, far from civilization, they were forced to fend for themselves. There were no helicopters to airlift the injured in case of an emergency, even if they could have afforded one. People of his generation either made it or they didn't. For example, Howard had his own home remedies, such as a cough medicine that called for a few drops of kerosene among other things. He even pulled his own teeth. Gary Cobb and Floyd witnessed an exhibition of this art, and the thought of it makes Gary shudder even today.

Howard once was offered a job in the woods and since he had to walk in to it, he arrived after everyone had gone to bed. In those days the men all bunked in one bed. Howard searched around for a hole in the mass of humanity and was about to pop in when he noticed that the man next to him had bed bugs crawling on his neck. Howard took a blanket and went out to the lean-to where the horses were stabled and slept there.

He also confessed that his family was so poor and so remote that he and a neighbor sat up the night his mother died and embalmed her with whatever was handy. Instead of formaldehyde they used mint and other herbs.

Equipped with this kind of background, Howard was not about to put up with the overbearing or pompous. When asked by an overstuffed sport why the black flies bit him and not Howard, the reply as:

"Those little bastards come on to some people like hyenas to a gut cart."

One day while Howard was on the gate, a stranger drove up and asked:

"Are you Howard Monroe?"

"So they tell me," replied Howard.

"Are you Howard *Estes* Monroe?" the stranger insisted.

"The one and the same," was the response.

"Well, so am I," said the stranger.

It seems that the two had been separated for many years and the son had come to the area to check gravestones to see if he could locate his father only to learn that the man in question was still living.

In 1977 when he was in his mid-80's, Howard fell off the back of a dump truck, cracking his hip and forcing him into the hospital. It was the final blow and he never came out. Charlie Reiche was one of the last people to visit Howard there and during their talk the phone rang.

"Now who in hell can that be," Howard muttered, "the undertaker?"

The Fauna of Pierce Pond

When *homo sapiens* takes it upon himself to move into the domain of the bear, the deer and the moose, he should remember at all times that he is the trespasser. If you were a bear and you saw a freshly baked banana cake resting on the sideboard near an open window, wouldn't you be tempted? And if you were Ruth Coffin of Lee and a bear came onto your kitchen porch, wouldn't you chase it off with a broom? Exactly. There are two sides to any question and sometimes *homo sapiens* wins and sometimes he loses. In the above instance he lost the cake, but won the war of the porch, as Maude Cobb will bear witness.

Deer are no problem, except that they can be seen in large numbers during the off season, but are not as easy to find once the law goes off in the fall.

At other times if bears get too familiar a camp operator can call in the game wardens who will trap the animals and carry them off to another neck of the woods.

Bears are often found around sporting camps because there is usually a dump nearby which contains remnants of food such as empty jam jars, corn cobs or the like. The smell of a baked pie or cake will attract *ursidae canavora* as readily as *homo sapiens* and seldom the twain should meet. In the early years of the Maude-Floyd era the numerous boys summering under the Cobbs' care got excited about the bear that was visiting the dump, so one night they planned to sneak out after the lights were turned off and go see for themselves.

Floyd, who had pretty keen ears, got wind of the plot and, in anticipation, took the mounted head of a bear from the dining room and hid it in the brush beside the road to the dump. When the youngsters came close enough, Floyd let out a growl and shoved the bear head out of the bushes. The reaction was instantaneous and spectacular. The kids wheeled and rushed back to camp.

When the truth came out, one victim said:

"I wasn't scared."

Whereas a second youngster replied:

"Maybe you weren't, but it scared the hell out of me."

In another incident, the bears did not make out as well. Dr. Covert of Kingfield found two cubs in the spring of 1960 and took them home as pets. By mid-summer he realized that he had made a mistake and tried to find a home for them. When he was unsuccessful he did the only thing he could: release them into the wilds. He left them off on the road to Pierce Pond. One wandered off towards a lumber operation, saw a worker and followed him right up onto a machine. Not knowing that the cub was used to humans and probably hungry, the worker eliminated the animal without asking any questions.

The second animal found its way to Lindsay Cove and for several days followed the tote wagon to and from the gate.

Curiosity got the better of the folks in camp and they went over to the cove to see the intruder, but in the meantime he had had a similar idea so that when the curious got back to camp the bear was sitting on the dock.

These adventures were occurring in raspberry time and as is the custom, the women in camp, after the noon business had been cleaned up, would go out to pick. Such is the rapidity of communications in the wilds of Maine, the Bangor Daily News was able to get a photographer to Pierce Pond in time to get a picture of Joan Cobb picking berries with the bear cub standing beside her calmly eating.

Of note is the experience of an English couple, who had been referred to Pierce Pond by the Fish and Game Department. The young bear tried to get into their boat at Lindsay Cove whereupon the visitor explained:

"Oh, but you don't have a reservation."

Then there was Slim, who went ashore while fishing to answer a call of nature. He had assumed the standard position when he suddenly saw the bear coming towards him. His retreat, suspenders at the unready, must have looked like a scene from a Mack Sennett comedy.

In due time Floyd realized that something had to be done with the cub, so he got two young fellows to take the bear up the lake and leave him. Getting the animal into the boat was easy enough but getting him out at the other end of the trip was something else. He liked humans; they fed him. Hence, when the young males would put him ashore he would climb back into the boat. Eventually they accomplished their mission and returned to camp. The bear cub did not go far. In fact, he kept trying to swim out to boats fishing in that part of the pond. Finally he caught Clare Bousquet as he worked his boat through the thoroughfare. Unfortunately Clare had his lunch in his coat pocket and the bear immediately tried to get it. Clare, thoroughly scared, pulled his knife and tried to finish off the animal. Leaving it for dead, Clare returned to camp to report the incident.

As soon as he was able, Floyd went up to the thoroughfare in order to bury the young bear, but was unable to find it. If the bear were alive it would be more dangerous than ever so Floyd went back to camp for his rifle. On his return, Floyd found the miserable cub and quickly ended its suffering.

Some progress has been made at Pierce Pond in respect to bears. Morgan Daboll, who holds the current record for longevity at the camp (54 years), recalls that Charles Mitchell often complained of having to repair the horse barn near the Basin every time a bear menaced the animals. Bears do not consider trucks and tractors as food.

Floyd's episode with the moose that got tangled in the telephone line ended much more pleasantly. As Floyd tells it:

"When the phone went out we naturally followed up the line and saw the trouble. We called the wardens and by the time they arrived the situation looked hopeless. The moose had the wire all around his horns, neck, body and legs. The wardens said immediately that there was one thing to do—shoot. Gary and I asked to let us try to free him and the wardens said:

"'Be our guests, but don't hold us responsible if anyone gets hurt.'

"Many of the guests from the camp came to watch as did

Howard Monroe, the gatekeeper, who provided much expert advice.

"We loaded the old dump truck with gravel and backed it into the woods as near to the moose as we could get. He could still range several feet before bringing up. Standing on the load of dirt, we rigged a large rope on a pole and attempted to get the rope around the antlers. I got off the truck to pick up the cutting pliers that had been dropped, and the bull, in a frenzy, made a lunge towards me. I barely made it under the truck. The antlers just grazed my arm—no damage.

"After securing the rope on his horns, we attached it to a pick-up truck and forcibly led the bull to the truck body from which we could reach him. We took our cutting pliers and went to work. At first the moose would lunge and nearly come onto the truck, but as we began to get some of the wire off his antlers, head and neck, he seemed to sense that we were helping him and he calmed down somewhat. Finally, by getting under the truck body, we were able to dodge out and cut one strand at a time from his body, feet and legs. To everyone's amazement, including our own, we managed to free a magnificent animal to roam the ridges and swamps again.

"After the rope was cut from his horns, he just stood there a short while. Then he shook his head, held it high, and went snorting over the ridge. It seemed as though he figured he had won another battle."

Morgan Daboll recalls that at times Pierce Pond was a sort of orphanage for wild creatures. He found a young fox being nursed by bottle in the kitchen one morning and later realized that this was probably the same animal that Clare Bousquet became accustomed to feeding fish. Whenever he caught a trash fish, such as a pickerel or chub, Clare would bring it back to camp and place it on a stump near his cabin. Invariably the fish was gone the next morning .

Maineacs of long standing, such as the Cobbs, assume that the taking of deer is one of their inalienable rights. Once it was a necessity, then it became a sport and finally, it has been reduced to an excuse to get out into the woods. Gary Cobb's grandfather, Bump, believed in the *Bible's* exhortation to "Train up a child in the way he should go; and when he is old, he will not depart from it." Accordingly, he began taking Gary deer hunting when the latter was ten years old, and Gary still enjoys the fall season as much as any time of the year. Gary's father, Floyd, continued the education of his son in the ways of the woods and Gary maintains that his father is the best hunter he has ever known.

Father and son made an unusually fine team for tracking down wounded deer. Many times have they listened to the tale of some frustrated hunter and then gone into the woods and found the signs that led them to the animal in question. Over the years they came to consider such experiences as tests of their woodsmanship. They also consider Pierce Pond and the Dead River country as prime hunting territory with plenty of ridges on which big bucks can roam. It is also remote, a feature that adds zest to nimrods. In fact, Gary admits that getting out into the woods is at least half of the fun of hunting.

The deer herd in the Dead River area was greatly reduced in the late 1960's when severe winters with deep snows caused many deer to die of starvation. At the same time coyotes began to establish themselves and the lumber companies began cutting in those areas in which the deer were accustomed to winter. Such cutting also brought in renegade wood cutters who shot some 20 animals in one month. These factors, plus an increase in the number of hunters, made it virtually impossible for the herd to grow. Floyd Cobb did his best to help by cutting cedar and putting it within reach of wintering deer. In time the authorities introduced such measures as the "bucks only" law and the issuance of doe permits. In recent years the herd has been making a comeback.

Pierce Pond is no place in which to have a heart attack, especially in late fall in the middle of a northeasterly snow storm, but such was the situation one year after two middle-aged deer hunters underestimated their situation. They had gone off in the morning to hunt Hurricane Mountain which lies north of the Upper Pond and why they stayed out so long will never be known. By the time darkness began to set in, the storm, a typical nor'easter, had been hard at it for two hours. Floyd and Gary and guide Alfred Marble were about to set off in search of the missing men when they heard the sound of a motor and shouts for help.

They ran down to the dock and faced a tragic situation. There in the bottom of the boat was one hunter, lying lifeless in four or five inches of snow and water. His partner was not much better off. As he was helped ashore he managed to explain that the heart attack came while they were crossing the Upper Pond and the survivor had done his best to get back to camp as soon as possible, but had become lost in the Middle Pond among the many islands. Eventually he worked his way along the shore and got clear. However, he had no idea of how long he was lost.

Dealing with death is difficult in any case, but when one is deep in the woods the problem is seriously complicated. First off, the sheriff and the medical examiner have to be brought in. That meant that Gary and Alfred Marble had to drive some seven miles to meet the officials, who wisely brought along an undertaker. Back seven miles to camp, where, after the body was examined, it was placed on a deer carrier in order to get it to the landing where the four-wheel-drive vehicle was waiting.

By this time the snow had reached a depth of a foot. Back seven miles to the vehicle the officials had used and finally the return trip to Pierce Pond. It was well after midnight when the adventure was over. Sleep did not come easily.

Another tragedy was averted in the deer season of 1988. Floyd Cobb, as is his custom since retirement, was in camp for a variety of reasons. First of all, his experience in the woods is invaluable to the deer hunters who come north each year. Secondly, he is a good cook and thirdly, he just loves to be at Pierce Pond to be close to his favorite sport. In this instance, it was his experience that paid off.

Sitting in camp while the rest of the party was off in the woods, Floyd began to realize that the wind on the pond was picking up quickly. It was mid-afternoon which meant that not much sunlight was left. He became nervous and looked up the pond in the direction four hunters had gone in the morning. The waters were boiling and Floyd realized that four hunters, heavily clothed, plus a deer or two, would have a difficult time trying to get back to camp. He did not hesitate long, and pulled on some heavy clothing.

As he launched a boat, Floyd realized that the wind was roaring across the pond from the southeast while his course was 90 degrees nearer north. In other words the wind would be on his starboard beam, making steering about as difficult as possible. Spray soon came over the starboard gunnel as wind and waves attacked the boat. Suddenly, about 400 yards out, Floyd spotted what looked like three blaze orange hats floating on the water. He had found his quarry, but was he too late?

Holding his course he soon got a better picture of the horizon and realized that he was not too late. What had looked like floating hats now turned out to be hunters clinging to an overturned boat. There still remained the problem of getting his guests aboard. Floyd was 70 years of age at this point and pulling three men, fully clothed, from the water was no child's play. Somehow he managed, despite his bobbing boat, and returned the half-frozen trio to the warmth and safety of camp.

There was still one hunter missing. He had failed to meet his companions at the appointed hour. As soon as Gary returned from guiding his guests, he immediately started a one-man expedition into the night, for it was now dark. Some six hours later, at 11p.m., Gary found his man under a spruce tree, resigned to spending the night in a driving rain storm.

One ordinarily does not think much about death at Pierce Pond. Most folks go there to escape unpleasantness and to enjoy life in the open. Such is the case in August when families with children are apt to be present. A few years back when a number of children were in residence, a young loon found its way into the dock. Gary, ever the teacher, seized the opportunity to give his small, and larger, guests a taste of nature. He found a box and put the loon in it. Then he gathered a group to go out on the pond and watch the return of the prodigal to its family.

Once on the water Gary steered the boat so as to be upwind of the adult loons when the offspring was put back in the water. Having released the bird he then maneuvered the boat so that his guests could get a good view of the reunion. Just before the young loon reached its elders they dove, strange behavior from the human point of view. Suddenly they exploded from the water, tossed the young bird into the air, attacked it, tore it apart and ate it. Gary had returned the victim to the wrong family.

The return trip to camp was made in silence.

The Flies

In the beginning there were worms and grasshoppers and spinners. Then came wet flies, and then streamers. The skill of the fisherman increased in direct proportion to the decline in the fish population, so that today guides and serious fishermen are entomologists at heart. They still use streamers, but dry flies and nymphs have replaced the smaller wet flies.

As Bob Witbeck wrote in an earlier chapter, it was legal to use worms as late as 1945 and while he blushes at the idea now, he had his best catches right after World War II. The greatest change in fishing techniques at Pierce Pond came in 1966-1967 when the bulldozers came in over Otter Pond Mountain to cut logging roads for the harvest of timber in that area. Over a period of five years the soft wood was cut and then the hardwood. All this activity opened up access to Pierce Pond and the plug and worm fishermen had a field day as did the French-Canadian lumberjacks who came to work and live in the area. A not very pleasant hearing was held at Bingham, but the law was changed, despite local opposition, so that the small ponds were limited to fly fishing only and Pierce Pond itself to artificial lures only. Gary Cobb lost some income to these conservation moves, for until 1964 or so he had been selling nightcrawlers for as much as $1.25 per dozen.

At the end of the 1800's wet flies were the thing on Pierce Pond. The *Durham Ranger,* a yellow and brown affair, was a favorite of Dr. W. H. Barrett of New York, who was considered one of the most successful fishermen to frequent Pierce and Otter Pond Camps. He also was partial to the *Jock Scott* fly, which had as many colors as Joseph's coat, including black and yellow floss body, silver tinsel ribbing, Golden Pheasant crest and scarlet tuff on the tail, black and white hackle and blue, yellow, scarlet and white wing with a jungle cock eye.

The *Epting* wet fly, designed by C. W. Epting, a member of the Kennebec Valley Club, had a yellow body and barred black hackle and gray mallard wing. The Epting and Barrett names were frequently mentioned in reports from Otter and Pierce Pond Camps, along with those of the rest of the club members such as Humphries, Williams and Talcott.

As early as 1887 Dame, Stoddard & Kendall's, the popular Boston fishing tackle retailer, was pushing such favorites as *Coachman, Silver Doctor, Parmachene Belle, Red Ibis, Brown Hackle* and *Professor,* as the ones to use in July, August and September.

Another wet fly of the early years that has disappeared is the *Undertaker,* which had a white wool body and black and white tail and wings. The name itself may have done it in.

The more familiar *Dusty Miller, Parmachene Beau* and *Belle, Royal Coachman* and *Grizzly King* were popular from 1900 to 1920 or thereabouts and sometimes doubled as dry flies with the application of grease. When fishing was slow, or, in some instances when not, wet fly fishermen used dropper flies, usually two placed about a foot apart from the fly on the end of the leader. A favorite combination featured a *Royal Coachman, Parmachene Belle* and *Montreal,* all dominated by red.

In the 1920's the streamer fly came into being in an attempt to imitate smelt. The most famous of these was the *Gray Ghost,* created by Carrie Stevens of Madison and Upper Dam. As she tells the story, she was inspired on the first day of July in 1924 to dress a streamer with gray wings to imitate a smelt and she left her housework undone in order to develop the idea. Having made the fly she promptly put it to the test from one of the aprons on the dam for which the town is named. In less than an hour she hooked and landed a six-pound, 13-ounce brook trout which she entered into a *Field and Stream* fishing contest. She won second place which was worth an oil painting by Lynn Bogue Hunt, but more than that she became famous and was inundated by orders for the *Gray Ghost,* the name later given to the fly by Mr. Frank Bugbee of Willimantic, Connecticut.

Mrs. Stevens also created two other well-known streamers, the *Colonel Bates,* named for Col. Joseph D. Bates, Jr. of Long-meadow, Mass, the fishing authority and author; and the *General MacArthur,* of Correigidor fame. Col. Bates knew Pierce Pond and his son Bruce has been a regular guest there for years.

The *Gray Ghost* soon had many imitators including the *Black Ghost* and the *Supervisor.* The latter was designed by Warden Joseph S. Stickney, who at one time was Supervisor of Wardens for Maine and a frequent visitor to Pierce Pond. He also brought out the *Warden's Worry,* which is as famous for its name as for its efficiency in catching trout and salmon.

Three other streamers with a Pierce Pond flavor are the *Nine-Three*, the *Ballou Special* and the *Parson Tom*. The *Nine-Three* was designed by Dr. J. Hubert Sanborn of Waterville and was so named because the first salmon it fooled in Messalonskee Lake, in Oakland, weighed nine pounds and three ounces. It was put together to imitate a smelt with dark back, lighter below, a silver belly and jungle cock eyes.

The *Parson Tom* was the creation of Iral Bean, a sort of Latter Day Rance Ham whose name is spread over five administrations of Pierce Pond Camps. It was a cross between the *Supervisor* and the *Gray Ghost* and had two blue and two gray saddle hackles.

Finally, the *Ballou Special* came from the brain of A. I. Ballou, Jr., a garage owner from North Dighton, Massachusetts who later moved to Litchfield. He came to Pierce Pond in the 1920's, staying at least a month each season in an effort to catch a 20-pound salmon. He never did, but he became a good friend of Ben Ames Williams, the famous author, who came to Pierce Pond for the peace and quiet, rather than for the fishing. The *Ballou Special* was designed for Pierce Pond, although the originator pretended it was for use at the mouth of the Songo River on Sebago Lake. He worked for many years perfecting the fly. He also is given credit for other maribou streamers, which he dressed on long-shanked single hooks for use when smelt were hugging the banks *en route* up stream. When the smelt were going the other way he preferred a short-shanked double hook.

Ballou took his fishing seriously to the extent that he

brought two guides with him, Dick Page for his wife, and Bob Martin for himself. Martin came from Belgrade and is remembered for both his loud voice, which has been described as sounding like a bull moose with a sore throat talking through gravel, and for his talent as an entertainer.

Also popular in the 30's and still effective today are the *Barnes Special* and the *Edson Tiger*. Lowell Barnes was a guide at Sebago and William Edson was a successful Portland fly tier.

Herbert L. Welch, of Mooselookmeguntic, in addition to creating the *Black Ghost Streamer* also originated several others, of which the *Kennebago Streamer* is perhaps most notable. He also was a taxidermist and there is a nine-pound trout, which he mounted, gracing the walls of the Pierce Pond dining room. It was caught by Paul Kukonen of Worcester, Massachusetts, noted angler and lecturer.

In his comprehensive book on flies and fishing, *Streamer Fly Tying and Fishing*, Col. Bates reveals correspondence he had with A. I. Ballou in regard to the *Black Ghost*, one of a few Maine designs that has gained a national reputation. Herb Welch had had Nellie Newton, a fly dresser working for the Percy Tackle Company of Portland, work out his design at the Boston Sportsmen's Show in 1927. In a letter to Col. Bates, Ballou stated:

"On my trips to Maine it was my custom to stop at the Percy Tackle Shop in Portland, and to spend several hours having dressed new types of streamer flies which I had developed during the winter. On one of these stops in 1927 Mr. Percy asked Nellie Newton to work with me. Nellie tied a fly with a black body and several white feathers and said it was called the *Black Ghost*. I didn't think much of it.

"I went on from Percy's to Thompson's Camps at the mouth of the Songo River (on Sebago Lake). I had been there ten or twelve days when one morning I pushed the boat out into the river and anchored. I hooked into a beautiful trout and had him up to the boat several times, but finally lost him. Just then a Mr. Merritt from Connecticut came along in his boat with his guide. He had seen me with the fish and shouted that it looked like a Pierce Pond trout. Just then he cast his fly about three feet from my boat and hooked a large fish. When he landed it he pulled up to my boat to use my scales. It was a nice, 5 1/2 pound trout and the fly was still in his mouth.

"When I stared at the fly, Mr. Merritt said, 'Do you want a copy of this fly, Mr. Ballou?' I said I didn't, but I asked him where he got it. He said he had stopped the day before at a place in Portland where they tied flies and bought half a dozen, but that he didn't think the fly had a name. I said it had a name all right and that it was a *Black Ghost*, the same fly that Nellie Newton had tied for me. After telling her that I didn't think much of it, and then seeing Mr. Merritt catch a 5 1/2 pound trout right under my boat with it, I swore I would never use one of those *Black Ghosts* as long as I lived, and I never have.

"As you know, it turned out to be one of the best streamers that ever was developed. I think Mr. Merritt gave it a big start by giving samples away."

Bob Witbeck has pinned the *Wulff* flies as being new in 1945, just as the war was ending. They, of course, were the invention of Lee Wulff about whom any fisherman who reads the magazines knows much. This was the beginning of the scientific era of fly fishing with new materials such as fiberglass

and graphite for rods and new ideas about entomology coming
into the picture. There was also a surge in interest in the
outdoors, which meant there were more fishermen. To catch a
trout or salmon on a dry fly became the thing to do because it
did less damage to the fish, which could be readily released
after the pleasure of fooling him had been had.

Among the favorite dry flies in addition to the *Wulffs,*
which are used in the larger sizes for the green drake and
Hexagenia hatches, and in the smaller versions for Mayflies, are
the *Hendricksons, Hornbergs, Quill Gordons, Adamses* and *Cahills,*
which approximate the early Mayfly and Stone fly, and the
Bivisibles, Irresistables and *Muddler minnows,* which seem to be
more effective in June.

Caddis fly imitations come in many shapes and sizes, even
down to #22 hooks, but they catch big fish. The *Elk Hair Caddis*
is quite popular in the smaller sizes, as are nymphs, when
Hexagenia is about to hatch or during the day.

No discussion of flies can be complete without mention of
the *Mickey Finn,* another fly of national stature. We are also
indebted to Col. Bates for information on its origins. Apparently it was an unnamed and unknown pattern until John
Alden Knight, of Williamsport, Pennsylvania, angler, author
and creator of the Solunar Tables, popularized it with his
writings. According to Knight he was invited to fish at a club
near Greenwich, Connecticut where his host offered him a
small bucktail that had been most effective in catching trout
from the Mianus River. It worked that day for Knight and again
later in Canada at the Mad River Club near Toronto. Knight
offered what was then known by its dresser, William Mills and

Son, as the *Red and Yellow Bucktail* to a club member who promptly caught a respectable trout with it. As the result of that success it was agreed by all concerned that the fly should be named the *Assassin,* but later Gregory Clark, a noted feature writer who was in on the party, decided *Mickey Finn* was more appropriate, and perhaps more exciting. And *Mickey Finn* it remains.

Naturally, opinions about flies are as diversified as a multinational corporation. Some fishermen want to match the hatch and others work with old reliables such as the *Doodle Bug,* which looks like nothing God ever created, but does the job. The theory behind this action is that the fly is an irritant and causes the fish to strike out of curiosity or even anger. For the neophyte, if you find a fly that works, stick with it, because your confidence will cause you to fish harder with it. It's like the golf pro who is more comfortable and more successful if he plays his wedge from 90 yards.

The Future

To look at the woodlands surrounding Pierce Pond, one might get the feeling that God was in heaven and all was right with the world. The feeling does not last when one investigates the land machinations that have gone before and are still going on. When we last discussed ownership of the area, the Manufacturers Investment Company had constructed a pulp mill at Madison and some of its officials had become interested in Pierce Pond as a sporting territory. Had they done as well with the mill as they did with putting salmon in the pond, history might have come out differently.

The pulp mill at Madison did not prove profitable, however, and changes were made. Colonel Payne, who appears to have been the dominant stockholder in the Investment Company, tried to improve the situation by bringing in Garret Schenck, an able paper maker from Rumford. At the time he was Vice President of International Paper Company. The next step was to form the Northern Development Company with the idea of putting a mill in the Millinocket area. The colonel purchased a goodly share of the stock of this company and before long wrapped up everything under the title of the Great Northern Paper Company. This made GNP the new owner of Pierce Pond. Eventually it made additional purchases of property so that it owned all of Pierce Pond Township with the exception of a certain area along the Dead River which still belonged to the state.

It must be understood that the ownership of woodlands in the State of Maine is a most confusing business. Since much of the land has never been staked out, ownership is labelled "undivided" and management of such is left to several companies that specialize in keeping owners advised as to where they stand financially. Thus, when Louis Calder, the prime owner of the Economy Corporation, died suddenly, his affairs were given to a trust for administration. One of the first steps was to survey and stake out the actual land owned by the company. Another move was to create the Kennebec River Pulp and Paper Company to run the mill at Madison.

This in turn brought about the harvesting of timber around the east side of Pierce Pond and Upper Pierce Pond which set the area back for a number of years and led to limitations to the fishing in the outlying ponds as well as Pierce Pond itself. Harvesting of timber produces roads, which cause intrusion.

By 1977 the Kennebec Pulp and Paper Company was having its problems so, with the help of the Maine Guarantee Authority, a state agency designed to create business, it sold the mill and the properties of what had been the Economy Corporation to T-P Property Corporation which had a mill in Pennsylvania called Penntech Papers.

The timing was not good. The paper industry was leveling

off, the mill and its machinery were about 90 years old and within a year T-P Properties, or Penntech, decided to close the mill and salvage what it could. When all was settled, Penntech was left with about 1,700 acres on the east bank of Pierce Pond including all of the islands. The other 4,000 acres to the north and west of the Upper Pond remained in the hands of the Maine Guarantee Authority as did the mill.

Once again a paper maker, this time from abroad, decided to make a go of the Madison mill and this time it succeeded. The Myllykoski Oy of Finland purchased the old mill from the Maine Guarantee Authority in 1978 and began operations. Three years later, with an assist from the *New York Times*, it built a new high-tech plant that has been humming ever since under the name of Madison Paper Industries. Ownership of the operation is divided 60-40 with the *Times* on the lower end of the scale.

Meanwhile Scott Paper Company took an option on the 4,000 acres held by the Maine Guarantee Authority and in 1983 traded 2,000 metric tons of fully bleached softwood pulp for the deed to the 4,000 acres. The pulp went to the new mill at Madison, in a sort of Tinkers to Evers to Chance double play.

That left Scott Paper Company holding the bulk of the western side of Pierce Pond and Penntech the owner of the eastern shore. There are two exceptions to this statement. In 1983 Scott Paper made a land swap with the Ware brothers, John and Roland, originally from Rockland. They owned a half interest in common and undivided interest in a parcel of land near Brassua Lake. Scott Paper Company in an effort to tidy up its holdings suggested that 210 acres of land, including Fernald and Pickerel Ponds, west of the Thoroughfare, be exchanged for the Brassua parcel and so the deal was made.

There are also some 700 acres of public land owned by the state. They lie north of High and Helen Ponds on Pierce Pond Mountain. Finally, there is a small lot of land near the outlet that was acquired in the early 1980's from Central Maine Power by the Appalachian Trail Conference for a shelter which may be seen from the Basin. In the summer of 1990, Scott acquired the public lot as a result of a major land swap between Scott and the state for land around Moosehead Lake.

It is to the credit of the many land owners involved with Pierce Pond, and to the operators of Pierce Pond Camps, that there has been friendly cooperation among them. In fact, there is evidence that there will be a great deal more cooperation in the future.

In September of 1989, John Feingold of the Trust for Public Lands came to Pierce Pond to consult with Gary Cobb. He had heard a rumor that Penntech was thinking of selling its land on the eastern shore and he was trying to protect the public's interest. What he was hoping to do was buy the property and hold it until some friendly organization could be persuaded to buy it and hold it in perpetuity. His visit started a chain of events that accomplished his purpose, but in a different way. Listening to Gary Cobb and John Feingold discussing the matter was a group of serious fishermen who were just as interested in the matter as the two principals.

The upshot of this was a meeting held in Portland on February 1, 1989. It was called by Gary and Peter Leslie and held at DeMillo's restaurant in Portland. More than 50 persons attended. Among them were Peter Leslie from Penntech,

Marc Johnson from Scott Paper Company, as well as Gary Cobb, John Feingold and a platoon of Pierce Pond fishermen. This meeting generated a smaller one less than two weeks later at which the Maine Wilderness Watershed Trust was formally and legally established.

A third meeting, held August 9, 1989 at Portland, produced some by-laws and a slate of four officers and directors for two years, four directors for one-year terms, four more for three year terms and an Advisory Board of seven. Officers included Robert Eastman, president, Fryeburg; Charles Burnham, Vice President, Durham, NH; Scott Hutchinson, Treasurer, Cumberland Foreside; and David F. Soule, Jr., clerk, Westport Island.

Directors for one year were Daniel Bell, Pownal; Pat Jackson, Jr., Yarmouth; Charles Abbe, Concord, NH; and Jerry Bley, Augusta. Directors for three years included Richard Pierce, Dixfield; Gerry Morton, North New Portland; Joe Wishcamper, Freeport; and Mrs. Wendy Gorman, Yarmouth. The Advisory Board is composed of Gary Cobb, North New Portland; Tim Harrison of Harrison's Camps, Bingham; Greg Drummond, North New Portland; Dr. Roland Ware, Portland; Bill Wing, Central Maine Power Company, Augusta; Peter Leslie, Cape Elizabeth; and Dennis Shaffer, representing the Appalachian Trail Conference, Norwich, VT. Bley, Pierce and Scott were appointed to a Lands Committee and Cobb, Drummond and Pat Jackson were named to the Membership Committee.

Seven months later, near the anniversary of its first meeting, the Membership Committee was able to report a paid membership of more than 500 and the Lands Committee dramatically arranged for the signing of an easement with Penntech Papers on the spot. John Leslie did the honors for Penntech and Charles Burnham for the Watershed Trust. Tom Colgan, Carl Van Husan and Donna Cassee of Scott Paper were among the 100 attending.

Specifically, the easement eliminated the possibility of further development on the 1,700 acres of property then owned by Penntech on the eastern shore of Pierce Pond in perpetuity, except for three lots that were reserved for the personal use of the principals. This was a major step forward by an organization that had been in business for only a year. It also bode well for the future, what with Dr. Roland Ware on the Board of Advisors and the Scott Paper Company having taken an active part in the proceedings to date.

In September of 1991 another step was taken toward the complete preservation of Pierce Pond when Charlie and Trudy Valentine of Norton, MA purchased the 1700 acres on the eastern shore of the pond from the Penntech Company. A year earlier the company had sold all of its properties to an Oregon company with the exception of the Pierce Pond piece. Even with the conservation easement in place there was concern that a new owner might not be as sensitive to the needs of the area as regular Pierce Ponders might wish. Fortunately, the Valentines are Pierce Ponders and have no plans for the property, other than protecting it.

Tied in with this transaction was the change in ownership of several islands in the pond. The Abbe family was able to acquire the island bearing its name and Gary and Betty Cobb were able to purchase the islands they had preveiously been responsible for leasing. They were also able to acquire the

Williams property across the pond from the camps.

In addition to the Valentines, the president of T. P. Properties, John Leslie, deserves considerable credit for the fortuitous
changes at Pierce Pond. Besides a sympathetic participation in
the easement process, he also instituted a management program for the 1700 acres that for the past three years has effec-
tively controlled camping and day use in the area.

Specifically, John Leslie engaged Allen Philpot, an Embden native, at Otter Pond Cove, the access point to Pierce Pond
from the east. Whoever said: "The public be damned" had a
point for unless it is held in check the public will quickly foul its
own nest. By controlling litter and preventing encroachment by
fishermen with mobile campers Philpot has greatlyimproved
usage by the public. He has been helped by Greg Drummond,
also engaged by Leslie. Greg was given the assignment of
keeping an eye on the rest of the eastern shore and especially the
islands.

With a membership of more than 650 and with Jerry Bley
installed as a paid executive director, the Maine Wilderness
Watershed Trust is operating at full throtle. The prospect of
complete protection of Pierce Pond and its environs is definitely within the realm of possibility.

Winners of the Perry-Doris Cup

	TROUT		SALMON	
1952	C. J. Bousquet	3-12	C. J. Bousquet	8-4
	W. S. Wickwire	3-12		
1953	Dr. W. G. Fraser	5-4	Dr. D. K. Lewis	5-12
1954	C. W. Wilson	4-4	Alfred C. Blake	5-4
1955	Dr. D. E. Newhall	4-8	C. W. Newbury	4-12
1956	Maj. A. R. Stickney	3-8	Alfred C. Blake	4-0
1957	Tom Haddock	7-10	G. A. Keeney	5-12
1958	Alfred C. Blake	7-4	Marcel Adams	4-12
1959	Roger Newton	5-8	Dr. Gus Kaufmann	6-0
1960	Alfred C. Blake	4-8	Dr. W. G. Fraser	4-5
1961	C. J. Bousquet	5-8	George Kelley	4-8
1962	J. G. Tucker	5-5	C. J. Bousquet	5-0
1963	Willie Jones	6-4	C. J. Bousquet	7-7
1964	Paul Sidney	5-3	Bob Rice	7-7
1965	Leon Johnson	4-5	Erastus Corning	7-2
1966	Al Rothfuss	6-6	Charles E. Reiche	4-10
1967	Alfred C. Blake	5-11	Emile Gaulien	5-0
1968	Tony Malevich	5-13	Erastus Corning	4-12

	TROUT		SALMON	
1969	Tony Malevich	5-10	Al Altavesta	6-3
1970	William Hyer	6-4	Tom Blake	3-15
1971	Charles E. Reiche	5-5	Erastus Corning	4-12
1972	Al Purvis	4-10	Bob Anderson	4-14
1973	Paul Lepore	5-2	Fran Whittle	3-13
1974	Fred Burnham	5-1	Ed Kluck	3-14
1975	Bruce Bates	4-9	Leon Spinney	4-0
1976	Dr. Elio Baldini	4-11	Robert Hall	4-7
1977	George Bailey	4-10	James Ray	4-3
1978	James Foss	3-14	Joe Burke	4-8
1979	Doug Taylor	6-4	David Bryant	4-1
1980	Peter Korotie	4-6	Dick Carpenter	4-5
1981	Charles E. Reiche	5-5	Bruce Manternach	4-8
1982	Ted Hitchcock	4-0	Paul Stanilonis	3-15
1983	Clarence Ellison	5-4	Richard Childs	3-4
1984	Dr. Frank Kropp	6-2	R. F. Rossner	4-7
1985	Dr. Ferris Ray	7-8	Richard Bennett	4-3
1986	Bob Anderson	6-6	John Whittall	5-15
1987	Robert Kennedy	7-8	Ted Hitchcock	4-10

At this point, the silver Paul Revere bowl which the Grieves had purchased for the annual competition had no more room for engraving, so a system of individual trophies was adopted. Winners since 1987 have been:

1988	Alfred Beaudette	4-15	Pete Kluck	5-8
1989	Norris Bond	5-0	Sweet Wm. Hanson	4-7
1990	Joe Sheffel, Jr.	4-13	Bucky Buchanan	3-4
1991	Fred Burnham	4-1	Victor Staknis	3-4
			Peter Lepore	3-4

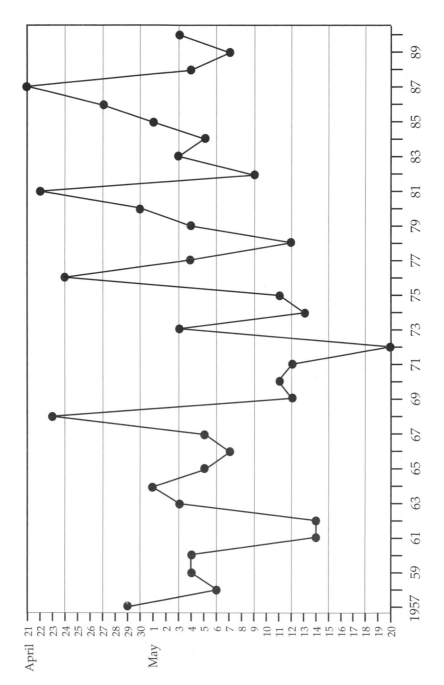

Dates of Ice Out, 1957 - 1990

Number of Board Fish, 1957-1990

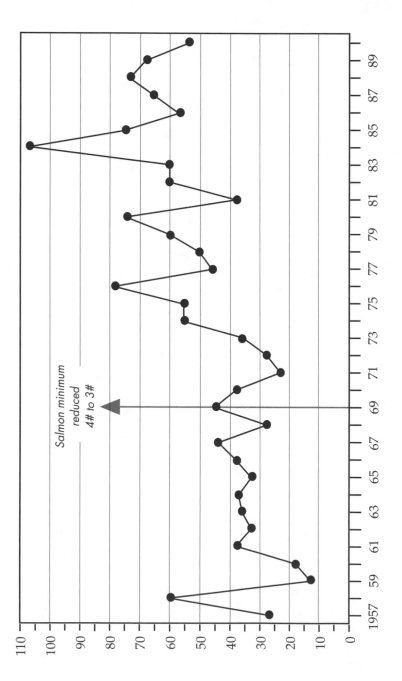

Summary of Board Fish, 1957-1990

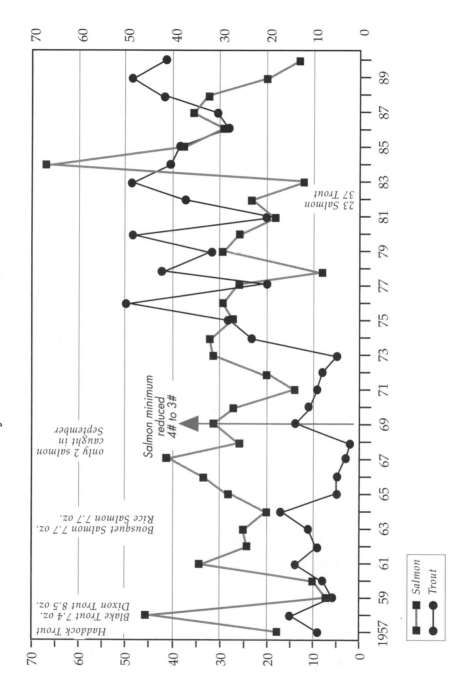

229

Maine Guides

A partial listing of Maine guides known to have worked
in the Pierce Pond and Dead River areas

At the Turn of the Century
> <u>Bingham and Moscow</u>
>> Rance Ham, John Morris, Jack Owens (to the 1930's),
>> Maurice "Dud" Prebel.
>
> <u>Caratunk and The Forks</u>
>> Ed Durgin, Frank Durgin *(Warden),* Ira Durgin, Ed
>> Dutelly (Jackman), Scott Hunnewell, Harry McGuire,
>> Lee Meservey, Tom Meservey, Bert Morris (to 1950's),
>> Dick Paige (to 1940's), Dave Pooler (to 1950's), Harry
>> Sands, Armond Spalding, Charles Spalding, George
>> Spalding, Harry Spalding.

1920's to World War II
> <u>Bingham and Moscow</u>
>> Robie Howes, Lescar Lawyerson (to 1950's)
>
> <u>Belgrade</u>
>> Frank Bickford, Lafayette Bushy, Wilkie Collins, Algie
>> Farnham, Varney Mosher, Harold Webster.

Caratunk and The Forks

Will Adams *(Warden),* Carl Bean, Guy Bean, Guy Berry (to 1950's), Iral Bean and Ural Bean (to 1960's), Hurbert Durgin, Sturgis Durgin (to 1950's), Walter Durgin, Tom Harris, Oscar Jones, Harold Martin, George McKinney, Henry McKinney, Charles Mitchell, Mark Morris, Al Nugent, William Powell, Hal Smith (to 1950's), Guy Temple.

Miscellaneous

Fred Daicey (Millinocket), Bob Martin (Auburn), Jim McKinney (Jackman), Elmer Merrill (Manchester).

World War II to 1980

Bingham and Moscow

Bunny Bean, Elden Bean, Bruce Gilbert, Allen Harriman, Verdell LaCasce (Solon), Ivan Lawyerson, Reggie McCollor, Dick Spalding.

Caratunk and The Forks

Hugh Comber, Joe Durgin, Bill McKay, Carroll York.

Dixfield

Ralph Griffin, Alfred Marble, Fern Mathieu (Lewiston), Charles Norris, Omer Richards.

Lee

Floyd Cobb, Gary Cobb, Richard Cobb, Rip Downs, Robert Mallett, Claude Scribner, Avon Staples.

North New Portland

Lester Arsenault, Stub Taylor

The Present

North New Portland

Andy Cobb, Greg Drummond, Mark Goodwin, Bill Howe, Shane Nichols.

Miscellaneous

Charles Gill (Portland), Chris Leo (Harmony), Dave Peppard (Richmond, *Warden)*, Paul Pono (Moscow), Steve Staples (Winthrop).

Charlie Norris was one of four Pierce Pond guides who went on to operate their own camps. Charlie, along with his good wife Ruth and their children, ran Kidney Pond Camps in Baxter State Park for a number of years until the lease was not renewed in 1987 by the Park Commission.

The other guides to become operators were Al Nugent, who established Nugent's Camps on Chamberlain Lake in the Allagash Region; Richard Cobb, Floyd's first cousin, who went on to Bosebuck Camps, near Wilson's Mills; and Robert Mallett, who later took charge of Moose Point Camps near Portage.

Bibliography

Agricultural Survey of Somerset County, S.L. Boardman, Augusta, 1860

Appalachian Trail, Ann Sutton, Philadelphia, PA, 1967

Archeology of Maine, Warren K. Moorehead, Andover, MA, 1922

Arnold's March from Cambridge to Quebec, James H. Smith, New York, NY, 1903

Churchward's Big Game and Fishing Guide, Bangor & Maine R. R., Bangor, 1898

William Bingham's Maine Lands, Publications of the Colonial Society of Massachusetts, Boston, MA, 1954

Carleton's State of Maine Sportsman's Journal, Augusta, 1906-10

The Life of Abner Coburn, Charles E. Williams, Bangor, 1885

Dawn over the Kennebec, Mary R. Calvert, Lewiston, 1983

East Carry Pond Camps Register, circa 1886-1930

Forest and Sea Power, Robert G. Albion, Hamden, CT, 1965

Freshwater Fisheries of the U. S., Report of the U. S.
    Commission of Fish and Fisheries, Washington, DC,
    1872-73

Global Climate Change, R. A. Houghton and G. M. Woodwell,
    Scientific American, April, 1989

The Golden Voyage, the Life of William Bingham, Robert C.
    Alberts, Houghton Mifflin, Boston, MA, 1969

The Great American Land Bubble, A. M. Sakolski, New York,
    NY, 1932

Moses Greenleaf, E. C. Smith, The DeBurrans, Bangor, 1902

History of the District of Maine, Judge James Sullivan,
    Augusta, 1795

History of Lumbering, Richard G. Wood, University of Maine
    Studies, Orono, 1935

History of Madison, Emma Folsom Clark, Madison ,
    1962

History of Maine, William D. Williamson, Glazier, Master
    and Company, Hallowell, 1932

History of the Maine Woods, Philip T. Coolidge, Bangor, 1963

The House of Baring in American Trade & Finance, Ralph W.
    Hidy, Harvard University Press, Cambridge, MA, 1949

*Information Respecting the History, Condition and Prospects of
    the Indian Tribes of the United States*, Henry R. Schoolcraft,
    Lippincott, Grambo and Company, six volumes,
    Philadelphia, PA, 1853-57

In the Maine Woods, Bangor and Aroostock R. R., Bangor, 1900-40

The Kennebec, Robert P. T. Coffin, Farr and Rinehart, New York, NY, 1937

The Kennebec Wilderness Awakens, Mary R. Calvert, Lewiston, 1986

Kennebec Yesterdays, Ernest E. Mariner, Colby College Press, Waterville, 1954

Madison Register, H. E. Mitchell and R. N. Randall, Kents Hill, 1903

Maine Farmers Almanac, D. Robinston, Camden, 1819-present

Maine Historical Society Proceedings, Portland, 1888

Maine Railroads, Edward E. Chase, Portland, 1926

Maine Register (and various other titles) Portland, 1820-present

Maine Sportsman, Bangor, 1893-1908

Maine Recreation, Augusta, 1930-31

Maine Fish & Game, Augusta, 1959-64

Maine Woods, Philips, 1869-1913

March to Quebec, Kenneth Roberts, Doubleday, Doran, New York, NY, 1938

The New York Times, 1895-1896

The Northern, John E. McLeod, Great Northern Paper Company, Millinocket, 1961 (Condensation)

Pine Trees & Politics, Joseph J. Malone, University of
    Washington Press, Seattle, WA, 1964

Pioneer Days of the Catholic Church in Maine, Maine Catholic
    History Magazine, Waterville

Propagation of Food Fishes, Report of U. S. Commissioner of
    Fish, Washington, 1874-75

Reports of Maine Fish Commission (later Department of Inland
    Fisheries & Game), Augusta, 1867-present

Skowhegan on the Kennebec, Louis Helen Coburn,
    Skowhegan, 1941

Charles Spalding Diary, 1899-1901

Sprague's Journal of Maine History, Dover, 1913-26

Streamer Fly Tying and Fishing, Col. Joseph T. Bates, Jr.,
    Stackpole Books, Harrisburg, PA, 1966

Ten Million Acres, Austin Wilkins, TBW Books, Woolwich,
    1978

Trending into Maine, Kenneth Roberts, Little Brown, Boston,
    MA, 1938

Yankee Logger, Steward H. Holbrook, International Paper
    Company, New York, NY, 1961